Cambridge English

IELTS 13

GENERAL TRAINING

WITH ANSWERS

AUTHENTIC EXAMINATION PAPERS

Cambridge University Press
www.cambridge.org/elt

Cambridge Assessment English
www.cambridgeenglish.org

Information on this title: www.cambridge.org/9781108555319

First published 2018

20 19 18 17 16 15 14 13 12 11 10 9 8 7 6 5 4 3 2 1

Printed in China by CNPIEC Beijing Congreat Printing Co.,Ltd

A catalogue record for this publication is available from the British Library

ISBN 978-1-108-60420-8 Academic Student's Book with answers with Audio for New Oriental School China reprint edition
ISBN 978-1-108-61941-7 Academic Student's Book with answers with Audio China reprint edition
ISBN 978-1-108-45049-2 Academic Student's Book with answers
ISBN 978-1-108-55309-4 Academic Student's Book with answers with Audio
ISBN 978-1-108-55531-9 General Training Student's Book with answers with Audio China reprint edition
ISBN 978-1-108-45055-3 General Training Student's Book with answers
ISBN 978-1-108-55319-3 General Training Student's Book with answers with Audio
ISBN 978-1-108-45067-6 Audio CDs (2)

Contents

Introduction

The International English Language Testing System (IELTS) is widely recognised as a reliable means of assessing the language ability of candidates who need to study or work where English is the language of communication. These Practice Tests are designed to give future IELTS candidates an idea of whether their English is at the required level.

IELTS is owned by three partners: Cambridge English Language Assessment, part of the University of Cambridge; the British Council; IDP Education Pty Limited (through its subsidiary company, IELTS Australia Pty Limited). Further information on IELTS can be found on the IELTS website www.ielts.org.

WHAT IS THE TEST FORMAT?

IELTS consists of four components. All candidates take the same Listening and Speaking tests. There is a choice of Reading and Writing tests according to whether a candidate is taking the Academic or General Training module.

Academic	General Training
For candidates wishing to study at undergraduate or postgraduate levels, and for those seeking professional registration.	For candidates wishing to migrate to an English-speaking country (Australia, Canada, New Zealand, UK), and for those wishing to train or study at below degree level.

The test components are taken in the following order:

Listening 4 sections, 40 items, approximately 30 minutes		
Academic Reading 3 sections, 40 items 60 minutes	or	**General Training Reading** 3 sections, 40 items 60 minutes
Academic Writing 2 tasks 60 minutes	or	**General Training Writing** 2 tasks 60 minutes
Speaking 11 to 14 minutes		
Total Test Time 2 hours 44 minutes		

GENERAL TRAINING TEST FORMAT

Listening

This test consists of four sections, each with ten questions. The first two sections are concerned with social needs. The first section is a conversation between two speakers and the second section is a monologue. The final two sections are concerned with situations related to educational or training contexts. The third section is a conversation between up to four people and the fourth section is a monologue.

A variety of question types is used, including: multiple choice, matching, plan/map/diagram labelling, form completion, note completion, table completion, flow-chart completion, summary completion, sentence completion and short-answer questions.

Candidates hear the recording once only and answer the questions as they listen. Ten minutes are allowed at the end for candidates to transfer their answers to the answer sheet.

Reading

This test consists of three sections with 40 questions. The texts are taken from notices, advertisements, leaflets, newspapers, instruction manuals, books and magazines. The first section contains texts relevant to basic linguistic survival in English, with tasks mainly concerned with providing factual information. The second section focuses on the work context and involves texts of more complex language. The third section involves reading more extended texts, with a more complex structure, but with the emphasis on descriptive and instructive rather than argumentative texts.

A variety of question types is used, including: multiple choice, identifying information (True/False/Not Given), identifying the writer's views/claims (Yes/No/Not Given), matching information, matching headings, matching features, matching sentence endings, sentence completion, summary completion, note completion, table completion, flow-chart completion, diagram label completion and short-answer questions.

Writing

This test consists of two tasks. It is suggested that candidates spend about 20 minutes on Task 1, which requires them to write at least 150 words, and 40 minutes on Task 2, which requires them to write at least 250 words. Task 2 contributes twice as much as Task 1 to the Writing score.

In Task 1, candidates are asked to respond to a given situation with a letter requesting information or explaining the situation. They are assessed on their ability to engage in personal correspondence, elicit and provide general factual information, express needs, wants, likes and dislikes, express opinions, complaints, etc.

In Task 2, candidates are presented with a point of view, argument or problem. They are assessed on their ability to provide general factual information, outline a problem and present a solution, present and justify an opinion, and to evaluate and challenge ideas, evidence or arguments.

Candidates are also assessed on their ability to write in an appropriate style. More information on assessing the Writing test, including Writing assessment criteria (public version), is available on the IELTS website.

Speaking

This test takes between 11 and 14 minutes and is conducted by a trained examiner. There are three parts:

Part 1

The candidate and the examiner introduce themselves. Candidates then answer general questions about themselves, their home/family, their job/studies, their interests and a wide range of similar familiar topic areas. This part lasts between four and five minutes.

Part 2

The candidate is given a task card with prompts and is asked to talk on a particular topic. The candidate has one minute to prepare and they can make some notes if they wish, before speaking for between one and two minutes. The examiner then asks one or two questions on the same topic.

Part 3

The examiner and the candidate engage in a discussion of more abstract issues which are thematically linked to the topic in Part 2. The discussion lasts between four and five minutes.

The Speaking test assesses whether candidates can communicate effectively in English. The assessment takes into account Fluency and Coherence, Lexical Resource, Grammatical Range and Accuracy, and Pronunciation. More information on assessing the Speaking test, including Speaking assessment criteria (public version), is available on the IELTS website.

HOW IS IELTS SCORED?

IELTS results are reported on a nine-band scale. In addition to the score for overall language ability, IELTS provides a score in the form of a profile for each of the four skills (Listening, Reading, Writing and Speaking). These scores are also reported on a nine-band scale. All scores are recorded on the Test Report Form along with details of the candidate's nationality, first language and date of birth. Each Overall Band Score corresponds to a descriptive statement which gives a summary of the English language ability of a candidate classified at that level. The nine bands and their descriptive statements are as follows:

9 ***Expert User*** – *Has fully operational command of the language: appropriate, accurate and fluent with complete understanding.*

8 ***Very Good User*** – *Has fully operational command of the language with only occasional unsystematic inaccuracies and inappropriacies. Misunderstandings may occur in unfamiliar situations. Handles complex detailed argumentation well.*

7 ***Good User*** – *Has operational command of the language, though with occasional inaccuracies, inappropriacies and misunderstandings in some situations. Generally handles complex language well and understands detailed reasoning.*

6 ***Competent User*** – *Has generally effective command of the language despite some inaccuracies, inappropriacies and misunderstandings. Can use and understand fairly complex language, particularly in familiar situations.*

5 ***Modest User*** – *Has partial command of the language, coping with overall meaning in most situations, though is likely to make many mistakes. Should be able to handle basic communication in own field.*

4 ***Limited User*** – *Basic competence is limited to familiar situations. Has frequent problems in understanding and expression. Is not able to use complex language.*

3 ***Extremely Limited User*** – *Conveys and understands only general meaning in very familiar situations. Frequent breakdowns in communication occur.*

2 ***Intermittent User*** – *No real communication is possible except for the most basic information using isolated words or short formulae in familiar situations and to meet immediate needs. Has great difficulty understanding spoken and written English.*

1 ***Non User*** – *Essentially has no ability to use the language beyond possibly a few isolated words.*

0 ***Did not attempt the test*** – *No assessable information provided.*

MARKING THE PRACTICE TESTS

Listening and Reading

The Answer Keys are on pages 117–124.
Each question in the Listening and Reading tests is worth one mark.

Questions which require letter / Roman numeral answers

- For questions where the answers are letters or Roman numerals, you should write *only* the number of answers required. For example, if the answer is a single letter or numeral you should write only one answer. If you have written more letters or numerals than are required, the answer must be marked wrong.

Questions which require answers in the form of words or numbers

- Answers may be written in upper or lower case.
- Words in brackets are *optional* – they are correct, but not necessary.
- Alternative answers are separated by a slash (/).
- If you are asked to write an answer using a certain number of words and/or (a) number(s), you will be penalised if you exceed this. For example, if a question specifies an answer using NO MORE THAN THREE WORDS and the correct answer is 'black leather coat', the answer 'coat of black leather' is *incorrect*.
- In questions where you are expected to complete a gap, you should only transfer the necessary missing word(s) onto the answer sheet. For example, to complete 'in the ...', where the correct answer is 'morning', the answer 'in the morning' would be *incorrect*.
- All answers require correct spelling (including words in brackets).
- Both US and UK spelling are acceptable and are included in the Answer Key.
- All standard alternatives for numbers, dates and currencies are acceptable.
- All standard abbreviations are acceptable.
- You will find additional notes about individual answers in the Answer Key.

Writing

The sample answers are on pages 125–132. It is not possible for you to give yourself a mark for the Writing tasks. We have provided sample answers (written by candidates), showing their score and the examiner's comments. These sample answers will give you an insight into what is required for the Writing test.

HOW SHOULD YOU INTERPRET YOUR SCORES?

At the end of each Listening and Reading Answer Key you will find a chart which will help you assess whether, on the basis of your Practice Test results, you are ready to take the IELTS test.

In interpreting your score, there are a number of points you should bear in mind. Your performance in the real IELTS test will be reported in two ways: there will be a Band Score from 1 to 9 for each of the components and an Overall Band Score from 1 to 9, which is the average of your scores in the four components. However, institutions considering your application are advised to look at both the Overall Band Score and the Bands for each component in order to determine whether you have the language skills needed for a particular course of study or work environment. For example, if you are applying for a course which involves a lot of reading and writing, but no lectures, listening skills might be less important and a score of 5 in Listening might be acceptable if the Overall Band Score was 7. However, for a course which has lots of lectures and spoken instructions, a score of 5 in Listening might be unacceptable even though the Overall Band Score was 7.

Once you have marked your tests, you should have some idea of whether your listening and reading skills are good enough for you to try the IELTS test. If you did well enough in one component, but not in others, you will have to decide for yourself whether you are ready to take the test.

The Practice Tests have been checked to ensure that they are of approximately the same level of difficulty as the real IELTS test. However, we cannot guarantee that your score in the Practice Tests will be reflected in the real IELTS test. The Practice Tests can only give you an idea of your possible future performance and it is ultimately up to you to make decisions based on your score.

Different institutions accept different IELTS scores for different types of courses. We have based our recommendations on the average scores which the majority of institutions accept. The institution to which you are applying may, of course, require a higher or lower score than most other institutions.

Further information

For more information about IELTS or any other Cambridge English Language Assessment examination, write to:

Cambridge English Language Assessment
1 Hills Road
Cambridge
CB1 2EU
United Kingdom

https://support.cambridgeenglish.org
http://www.ielts.org

Test 1

LISTENING

SECTION 1 *Questions 1–10*

Complete the table below.

*Write **ONE WORD AND/OR A NUMBER** for each answer.*

COOKERY CLASSES

Cookery Class	Focus	Other Information
Example The Food ....Studio........	how to **1** .... and cook with seasonal products	• small classes • also offers **2** .... classes • clients who return get a **3** .... discount
Bond's Cookery School	food that is **4**	• includes recipes to strengthen your **5** .... • they have a free **6** .... every Thursday
The **7** .... Centre	mainly **8** .... food	• located near the **9** .... • a special course in skills with a **10** .... is sometimes available

SECTION 2 *Questions 11–20*

Questions 11–13

*Choose the correct letter, **A**, **B** or **C**.*

Traffic Changes in Granford

11 Why are changes needed to traffic systems in Granford?

A The number of traffic accidents has risen.
B The amount of traffic on the roads has increased.
C The types of vehicles on the roads have changed.

12 In a survey, local residents particularly complained about

A dangerous driving by parents.
B pollution from trucks and lorries.
C inconvenience from parked cars.

13 According to the speaker, one problem with the new regulations will be

A raising money to pay for them.
B finding a way to make people follow them.
C getting the support of the police.

Questions 14–20

Label the map below.

*Write the correct letter, **A–I**, next to Questions 14–20.*

Proposed traffic changes in Granford

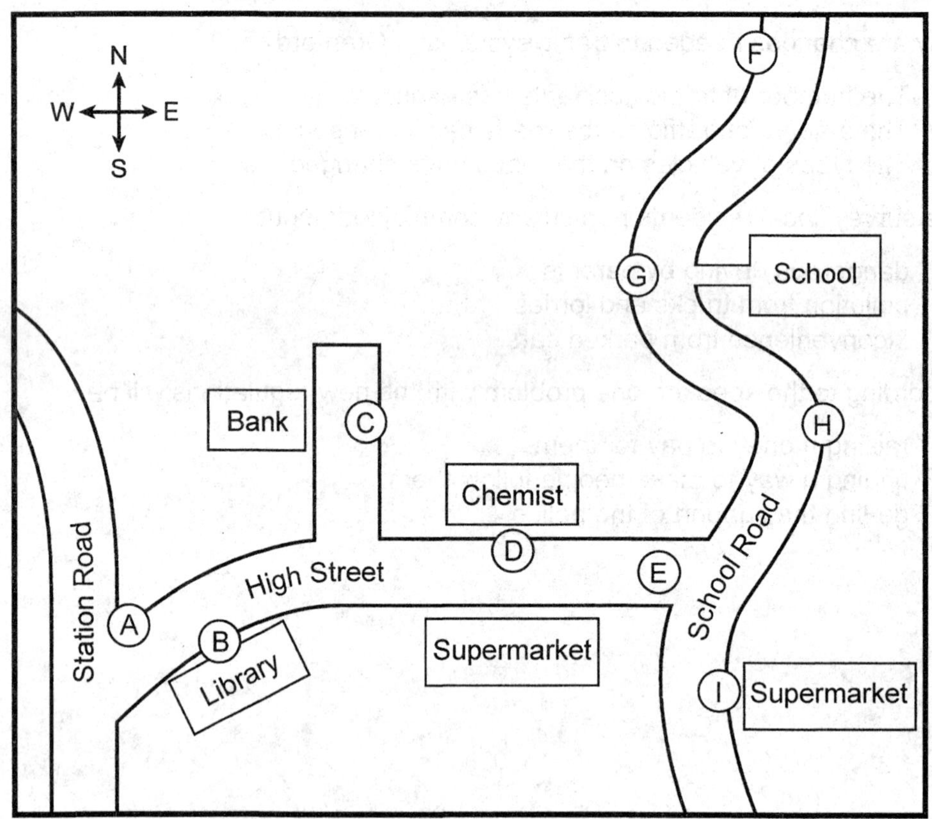

14 New traffic lights ....

15 Pedestrian crossing ....

16 Parking allowed ....

17 New 'No Parking' sign ....

18 New disabled parking spaces ....

19 Widened pavement ....

20 Lorry loading/unloading restrictions ....

SECTION 3 *Questions 21–30*

Questions 21–25

*Choose the correct letter, **A**, **B** or **C**.*

21 Why is Jack interested in investigating seed germination?

A He may do a module on a related topic later on.
B He wants to have a career in plant science.
C He is thinking of choosing this topic for his dissertation.

22 Jack and Emma agree the main advantage of their present experiment is that it can be

A described very easily.
B carried out inside the laboratory.
C completed in the time available.

23 What do they decide to check with their tutor?

A whether their aim is appropriate
B whether anyone else has chosen this topic
C whether the assignment contributes to their final grade

24 They agree that Graves' book on seed germination is disappointing because

A it fails to cover recent advances in seed science.
B the content is irrelevant for them.
C its focus is very theoretical.

25 What does Jack say about the article on seed germination by Lee Hall?

A The diagrams of plant development are useful.
B The analysis of seed germination statistics is thorough.
C The findings on seed germination after fires are surprising.

Questions 26–30

Complete the flow-chart below.

*Choose **FIVE** answers from the box and write the correct letter, **A–H**, next to Questions 26–30.*

A	container	**B**	soil	**C**	weight	**D**	condition
E	height	**F**	colour	**G**	types	**H**	depths

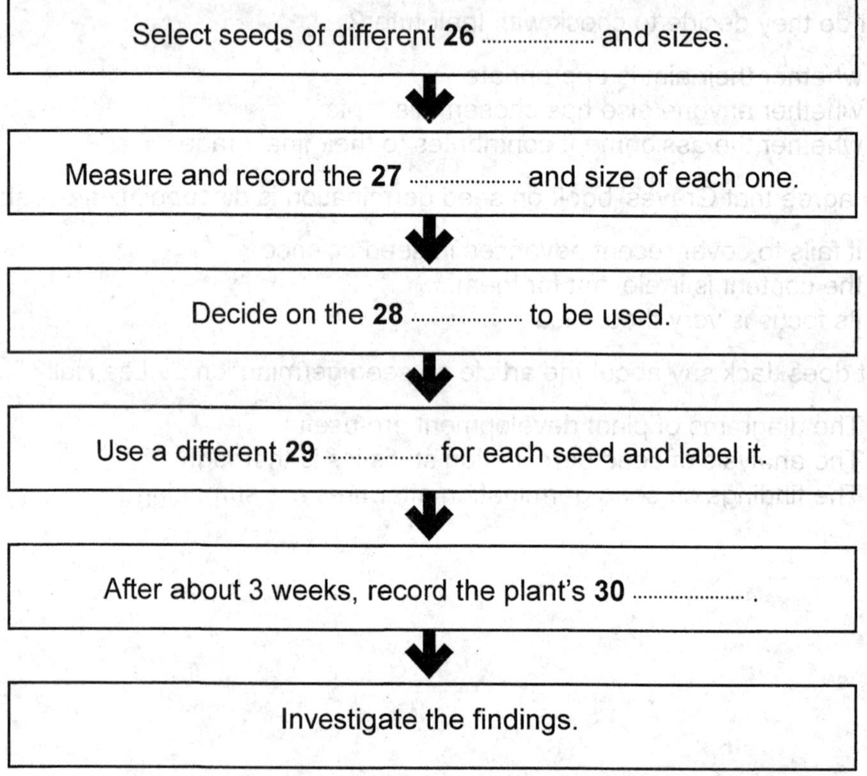

SECTION 4 *Questions 31–40*

Complete the notes below.

*Write **ONE WORD ONLY** for each answer.*

Effects of urban environments on animals

Introduction

Recent urban developments represent massive environmental changes. It was previously thought that only a few animals were suitable for city life, e.g.

- the **31** ………………………… – because of its general adaptability
- the pigeon – because walls of city buildings are similar to **32** …………………………

In fact, many urban animals are adapting with unusual **33** ………………………… .

Recent research

- Emilie Snell-Rood studied small urbanised mammal specimens from museums in Minnesota.
  - She found the size of their **34** ………………………… had increased.
  - She suggests this may be due to the need to locate new sources of **35** ………………………… and to deal with new dangers.
- Catarina Miranda focused on the **36** ………………………… of urban and rural blackbirds.
  - She found urban birds were often braver, but were afraid of situations that were **37** ………………………… .
- Jonathan Atwell studies how animals respond to urban environments.
  - He found that some animals respond to **38** ………………………… by producing lower levels of hormones.
- Sarah Partan's team found urban squirrels use their **39** ………………………… to help them communicate.

Long-term possibilities

Species of animals may develop which are unique to cities. However, some changes may not be **40** ………………………… .

READING

SECTION 1 *Questions 1–14*

Read the text below and answer Questions 1–7.

THE BEST SUITCASES

A Briggs and Riley Weekender

A weekend suitcase that's sophisticated and unusually spacious for its type. The strong nylon outer fabric is water and abrasion resistant, so it should handle any knocks without showing signs of damage.

B Mulberry Scotchgrain

Trimmed in brown leather, with gold details, this bag from the renowned fashion house is a truly indulgent buy. If you're investing this much in a suitcase then you'd better be planning an amazing holiday to go with it.

C Rimova Salsa

A design you can trust, this case is built from super light polycarbonate and is incredibly solid. The built-in combination lock offers state-of-the-art security so you can travel with peace of mind.

D Tripp Holiday

Simple and affordable, the Tripp range offers a great selection of tough cases. They also come in a huge range of cheerful colours that should go with anything you choose to put on, and you'll definitely be able to spot it on the luggage carousel at the airport.

E Eastpak Tranverz Holdall

For those who want something in between an annual holiday suitcase and a weekend bag, this is a fantastic compromise. With two wheels and a telescopic handle, the bag is guaranteed for 30 years. Did we mention it also comes in colourful leopard print?

F Herschel Parcel

From the brand behind some of today's most popular rucksacks, this suitcase really is a delight. Custom printed, with Herschel's signature leather toggles this well-crafted case is as cool, stylish and up to date as they come.

G The Diplomat

Travel in style with this beautiful suitcase that goes back to the days when trains ran on steam and air travel was leisurely. The leather case, part of the Steamline Luggage range, features roller wheels and a metal frame to hold it in shape.

Questions 1–7

Look at the seven reviews of suitcases, ***A–G****, on page 16.*

For which suitcase are the following statements true?

Write the correct letter, ***A–G****, in boxes 1–7 on your answer sheet.*

NB *You may use any letter more than once.*

1 This suitcase is for those who wish to purchase expensive luggage.

2 This suitcase is the right one for people who like to follow the latest fashion.

3 It is easy to choose one of these suitcases to match most clothing.

4 The manufacturer is confident that this suitcase will last a long time.

5 Items in this suitcase will not be affected if it gets wet.

6 This suitcase is of a useful, medium size.

7 Those who want to be reminded of an earlier age of travel will like this suitcase.

Read the text below and answer Questions 8–14.

THE OXFORD SCHOOL OF DRAMA

One-Year Acting Course

This is an intensive course which is designed for those who have completed their academic studies and have some theatre or film experience already. In order to be accepted you should be a high achiever, knowledgeable about the industry and determined to succeed.

Term One: Technical classes in acting, voice, movement, applied movement and characterisation, music, singing, film, radio and professional development. The term finishes with an internal production given for tutors and students.

Term Two: All technical classes continue from term one. There is an internal performance of a one-act play, the recording of an audio showreel at a professional studio and the Showcase Drama in front of an invited audience including casting directors and agents.

Term Three: Technical classes continue with additional focus on audition technique, workshops and masterclasses. This term includes a public performance of a play outdoors in the grounds of Blenheim Palace, and the chance to act a short film recorded on location by a professional crew.

How to Apply

Entry to The Oxford School of Drama is by audition only and there are no academic requirements for any of our courses.

Once we have received your application form and audition fee, we will email you with a date for your audition and further details about what to expect when you are here.

For your initial audition, you will need to prepare two contrasting speeches from plays, lasting no longer than two minutes. There will also be some group work for which you will need to wear loose, comfortable clothing.

If you are applying from overseas, you will be able to submit your first audition by means of DVD, YouTube or link to a secure website. You will be invited to submit this once we have received your application form and audition fee. If you are successful in your first audition, you will be invited to attend future auditions here at the school. The school will provide a free bus from central Oxford for those attending auditions.

Questions 8–14

Do the following statements agree with the information given in the text on page 18?

In boxes 8–14 on your answer sheet, write

TRUE *if the statement agrees with the information*
FALSE *if the statement contradicts the information*
NOT GIVEN *if there is no information on this*

8 Students can begin the one-year course without any previous involvement in acting.

9 Students will act in a performance in front of their classmates at the end of the first term.

10 Family members may attend a performance during the second term.

11 Students are required to make a film on their own in the last term of the course.

12 In their first audition, candidates perform speeches they have worked on in advance.

13 The Oxford School of Drama will send candidates details of local accommodation.

14 Overseas candidates can do all their auditions via a digital link.

SECTION 2 *Questions 15–27*

Read the text below and answer Questions 15–20.

BORDER CROSSING FOR COMMERCIAL VEHICLES

This Border Crossing Guide is designed for drivers and motor carriers operating commercial vehicles at Michigan's international border crossings. This information will help you cross the border from the US into Canada, and from Canada into the US.

Your first point of contact at the border consists of Primary Inspection. The best way to clear customs at Primary Inspection is to make sure Customs gets information about your shipment before you set off, using the Pre-Arrival Processing System (PAPS). When using this you need to provide information about your shipment, and you also need to send proof of a current annual inspection for your vehicle, tractor and trailer.

Before you arrive at the border, make sure you have all your paperwork up to date and ready to present at Primary Inspection. You'll need a photo ID in addition to your birth certificate or passport. Drivers must also turn on interior cab lights and open all interior drapes or blinds to sleeper areas for easy inspection.

If all of your paperwork is in order and was processed ahead of time, you will be released at the primary lane and this may be your only stop. If you are not a Canadian or US citizen, a visa is obligatory and you will also be required to complete an I-94 card. I-94 cards are available only at border crossings into the United States. Drivers who clear customs at Primary Inspection will be instructed to report to Immigration to fill out the I-94 card and receive verbal clearance from a US official to proceed into the United States. The charge for the I-94 card is $6.

If your paperwork is not in order, you will be directed to Secondary Inspection. When you get there, look for the signs for Truck Inspection and follow these.

Questions 15–20

Complete the flow-chart below.

Choose **NO MORE THAN TWO WORDS** *from the text for each answer.*

Write your answers in boxes 15–20 on your answer sheet.

Procedure for border crossing

Before setting off

To speed up the border crossing, use PAPS.

For this, send your **15** .... details and current vehicle inspection documents.

▼

Before arriving at the border

Check that documents such as **16** .... and birth certificate/passport are ready for inspection.

Make sure the **17** .... are on inside the vehicle.

Check that the **18** .... in the vehicle can be easily seen.

▼

At the border (Primary Inspection)

This may be the only stop if paperwork is in order.

Non US/Canadian citizens must have a visa, and go to

the **19** .... area to complete an I-94 card (there is a

small **20** .... for this) and to receive verbal clearance.

▼

At the border (Secondary Inspection)

If there is a problem with paperwork, you will be sent to Truck Inspection.

Read the text below and answer Questions 21–27.

Appendix: Dealing with absence in the workplace

This appendix considers how to handle problems of absence and gives guidance about authorised and unauthorised absence of employees from work.

The organisation should be aware of the rights of employees and in particular the requirements of the Equality Act 2010 when making any decisions about absences of employees who are disabled. In these cases the employer should consider what reasonable adjustments could be made in the workplace to help the employee. This might be something as simple as supplying an appropriate chair for the use of the employee. In cases where an employee suffers from an allergy caused by something in the workplace, the employer should consider remedial action or a transfer to alternative work.

If the absence is because of temporary difficulties relating to dependants, the employee may be entitled to have time off under the provisions of the Employment Rights Act 1996. In cases where the employee has difficulty managing both work and home responsibilities, employees have the right to request flexible ways of working, such as job-sharing, and employers must have a good business reason for rejecting any such application.

Employers should investigate unexpected absences promptly and the employee should be asked for an explanation at a return-to-work interview. In order to show both the employee concerned and other employees that absence is regarded as a serious matter and may result in dismissal, it is very important that persistent absence is dealt with firmly and consistently. Records showing lateness and the duration of and explanations for all spells of absence should be kept to help monitor levels of absence or lateness. If the employer wishes to contact the employee's doctor for more information about a medical condition, he or she must notify the employee in writing that they intend to make such an application and they must secure the employee's consent in writing. Consideration should be given to introducing measures to help employees, regardless of status or seniority, who may be suffering from stress. The aim should be to identify employees affected and encourage them to seek help and treatment.

Questions 21–27

Complete the notes below.

Choose ***ONE WORD ONLY*** *from the text for each answer.*

Write your answers in boxes 21–27 on your answer sheet.

Absence in the workplace

Employees' rights

- help with issues related to disabilities, e.g. provision of a suitable **21** ....
- provision of arrangements to deal with any work-related **22** ....
- time off work to deal with short-term problems of **23** ....
- possibility of arrangements that are **24** .... to help with domestic responsibilities

Recommendations to employers

- make it clear that absence is a possible reason for **25** ....
- ask employees for consent before contacting their **26** ....
- identify employees affected by **27** .... and provide support

SECTION 3 *Questions 28–40*

Questions 28–36

The text on pages 25 and 26 has nine paragraphs, **A–I**.

Choose the correct heading for each paragraph from the list of headings below.

*Write the correct number, **i–xi**, in boxes 28–36 on your answer sheet.*

List of Headings

i	Various sources of supplies
ii	The effects of going outside
iii	Oymyakon past and present
iv	A contrast in the landscape
v	Animals that can survive the cold
vi	How Oymyakon is affected by its location
vii	Keeping out the cold
viii	Not the only challenging time of the year
ix	Better than its reputation
x	Very few facilities in buildings
xi	More snow than anywhere else in the world

28 Paragraph A

29 Paragraph B

30 Paragraph C

31 Paragraph D

32 Paragraph E

33 Paragraph F

34 Paragraph G

35 Paragraph H

36 Paragraph I

A visit to Oymyakon, the world's coldest town

A You don't need a sat nav to drive to Oymyakon. From Yakutsk you cross the Lena River and simply follow the M56 almost all of the way before taking a left at Tomtor for the final few kilometres. The journey takes two days of hard driving; two days of glistening landscapes, frozen rivers and untouched snow; two days of endless forest and breathtaking beauty; two days to penetrate the heart of Siberia and reach the coldest inhabited place on Earth. The beauty surprised me. Siberia isn't known for its pleasant appearance. It's always billed as a place of hardship. But for hour after hour, the wintry wonderland was bathed in a crisp, clean sunshine, presenting a continuous panorama of conifer trees wreathed in silence and snow.

B As we left the flat plain, the road began to twist and turn, leading us into untouched hills and on towards the Verkhoyansk Mountains. Beneath their snow-clad peaks, the slopes became steeper and the valleys deeper. Down in a valley, we stopped to look at a hot spring beside the road. It was immediately obvious against the snow – a spot shrouded in heavy mist. Trees emerged from the strange haze as ghostly silhouettes.

C Despite the magical ambience of the Siberian wilderness, its reputation for hardship hit me every time I climbed out of the vehicle. Within less than a minute, the skin all over my face began to feel as if it were burning. If I wasn't wearing my two sets of gloves, I rapidly lost the feeling in my fingertips. I learned very quickly not to draw too deep a breath because the shock of the cold air in my lungs invariably set me off on an extended bout of coughing. Siberia in winter is a world barely fit for human habitation. This is a place of such searing cold that it bites through multiple layers of clothing as if they aren't there.

D Oymyakon is a quiet little town – the world's coldest – of about 550 inhabitants, with its own power station, a school, two shops and a small hospital. It probably originated as a seasonal settlement where reindeer herders spent the summer on the banks of the Indigirka River.

E The temperature when I arrived was -45°C – not particularly cold, I was informed. A number of factors combine to explain Oymyakon's record low temperatures. It is far from the ocean, with its moderating effect on air temperature. In addition, the town sits in a valley, below the general level of the Oymyakon Plateau, which, in turn, is enclosed on all sides by mountains up to 2,000 metres in height. As the cold air sinks, it accumulates in the valley, with little wind to disturb it. Oymyakon's average temperature in January is -50°C. Lower temperatures have been recorded in Antarctica, but there are no permanent inhabitants there.

F Day-to-day life in Oymyakon presents certain challenges during the long winters. There are hardly any modern household conveniences. Water is hacked out of the nearby river as great chunks of ice and dragged home on a sledge. The giant ice cubes are stacked outdoors and carried into the house one at a time to melt when needed. The lack of running water also means no showers or baths, or indeed flushing toilets. Since 2008, the town's school has enjoyed the luxury of indoor toilets, however. It's one of the small number of civic buildings in the centre of town that are linked to the power station.

G The power station provides winter heating in the form of hot water, but many houses lie outside its range and rely on their own wood-burning stove. Fuel is plentiful enough in the surrounding forest, but someone still has to venture out to cut the wood. Everybody in Oymyakon owns good boots, a hat made of animal fur and fur-lined mittens. The boots are usually made from reindeer hide, which is light but keeps your feet very warm – the individual hairs are hollow, like a thin tube with air inside. Since air is a poor conductor of heat, the skin makes excellent winter footwear, and felt soles give added insulation. Hats come in a variety of furs, including fox, raccoon, sable and mink.

H Oymyakon's two shops keep a decent stock of basic foods in tins and packets, but locals also have do-it-yourself options, including hunting, trapping, ice-fishing, reindeer-breeding and horse-breeding. Indeed, being self-sufficient runs in the blood in Siberia. The Oymyakon diet relies heavily on meat for its protein, a primary source of energy in the prolonged winter. Unsurprisingly, given the weather, everyone eats heartily in Oymyakon. A typical meal I was offered consisted of a thick horse soup and huge piles of horse meatballs, all washed down with cloudberry cordial.

I Spring is the best season here, I'm told. The snow melts, the river flows once more and the forest is full of wild flowers. But it's short. In the summer Oymyakon can be uncomfortably hot. Much of the forest becomes boggy, so mosquitoes are a constant presence. Oymyakon's climate certainly wouldn't suit me, but residents I spoke to said they wouldn't live anywhere else.

Questions 37–40

Complete the summary below.

Choose **ONE WORD ONLY** *from the text for each answer.*

Write your answers in boxes 37–40 on your answer sheet.

Why Oymyakon gets so cold

Oymyakon is a long way from any **37** .... which would prevent the temperature from falling so low. The town is located in a **38** .... within a plateau surrounded by **39** .... Because there is not much **40** .... , cold air collects in the town.

WRITING

WRITING TASK 1

You should spend about 20 minutes on this task.

You work for an international company, and would like to spend six months working in its head office in another country.

Write a letter to your manager. In your letter

- ***explain why you want to work in the company's head office for six months***
- ***say how your work could be done while you are away***
- ***ask for his/her help in arranging it***

Write at least 150 words.

You do **NOT** need to write any addresses.

Begin your letter as follows:

Dear .... ,

WRITING TASK 2

You should spend about 40 minutes on this task.

Write about the following topic:

> ***In some areas of the US, a 'curfew' is imposed, in which teenagers are not allowed to be out of doors after a particular time at night unless they are accompanied by an adult.***
>
> ***What is your opinion about this?***

Give reasons for your answer and include any relevant examples from your own knowledge or experience.

Write at least 250 words.

SPEAKING

PART 1

The examiner asks the candidate about him/herself, his/her home, work or studies and other familiar topics.

EXAMPLE

Television programmes

- Where do you usually watch TV programmes/shows? [Why?/Why not?]
- What's your favourite TV programme/show? [Why?]
- Are there any programmes/shows you don't like watching? [Why?/Why not?]
- Will you will watch more or fewer TV programmes/shows in the future? [Why?/Why not?]

PART 2

Describe someone you know who has started a business.

You should say:
who this person is
what work this person does
why this person decided to start a business
and explain whether you would like to do the same kind of work as this person.

You will have to talk about the topic for one to two minutes. You have one minute to think about what you are going to say. You can make some notes to help you if you wish.

PART 3

Discussion topics:

Choosing work

Example questions:
What kinds of jobs do young people not want to do in your country?
Who is best at advising young people about choosing a job: teachers or parents?
Is money always the most important thing when choosing a job?

Work–Life balance

Example questions:
Do you agree that many people nowadays are under pressure to work longer hours and take less holiday?
What is the impact on society of people having a poor work–life balance?
Could you recommend some effective strategies for governments and employers to ensure people have a good work–life balance?

Test 2

SECTION 1 *Questions 1–10*

Complete the notes below.

Write ***ONE WORD AND/OR A NUMBER*** *for each answer.*

South City Cycling Club

Example
Name of club secretary: Jim ....*Hunter*........

Membership

- Full membership costs $260; this covers cycling and **1** .... all over Australia
- Recreational membership costs $108
- Cost of membership includes the club fee and **2** ....
- The club kit is made by a company called **3** ....

Training rides

- Chance to improve cycling skills and fitness
- Level B: speed about **4** .... kph
- Weekly sessions
  – Tuesdays at 5.30 am, meet at the **5** ....
  – Thursdays at 5.30 am, meet at the entrance to the **6** ....

Further information

- Rides are about an hour and a half
- Members often have **7** .... together afterwards
- There is not always a **8** .... with the group on these rides
- Check and print the **9** .... on the website beforehand
- Bikes must have **10** ....

SECTION 2 *Questions 11–20*

Questions 11–16

*Choose the correct letter, **A**, **B** or **C**.*

Information on company volunteering projects

11 How much time for volunteering does the company allow per employee?

A two hours per week
B one day per month
C 8 hours per year

12 In feedback almost all employees said that volunteering improved their

A chances of promotion.
B job satisfaction.
C relationships with colleagues.

13 Last year some staff helped unemployed people with their

A literacy skills.
B job applications.
C communication skills.

14 This year the company will start a new volunteering project with a local

A school.
B park.
C charity.

15 Where will the Digital Inclusion Day be held?

A at the company's training facility
B at a college
C in a community centre

16 What should staff do if they want to take part in the Digital Inclusion Day?

A fill in a form
B attend a training workshop
C get permission from their manager

Questions 17 and 18

*Choose **TWO** letters, **A–E**.*

What **TWO** things are mentioned about the participants on the last Digital Inclusion Day?

A They were all over 70.
B They never used their computer.
C Their phones were mostly old-fashioned.
D They only used their phones for making calls.
E They initially showed little interest.

Questions 19 and 20

*Choose **TWO** letters, **A–E**.*

What **TWO** activities on the last Digital Inclusion Day did participants describe as useful?

A learning to use tablets
B communicating with family
C shopping online
D playing online games
E sending emails

SECTION 3 *Questions 21–30*

Questions 21–25

Choose the correct letter, ***A***, ***B*** *or* ***C***.

Planning a presentation on nanotechnology

21 Russ says that his difficulty in planning the presentation is due to

A his lack of knowledge about the topic.
B his uncertainty about what he should try to achieve.
C the short time that he has for preparation.

22 Russ and his tutor agree that his approach in the presentation will be

A to concentrate on how nanotechnology is used in one field.
B to follow the chronological development of nanotechnology.
C to show the range of applications of nanotechnology.

23 In connection with slides, the tutor advises Russ to

A talk about things that he can find slides to illustrate.
B look for slides to illustrate the points he makes.
C consider omitting slides altogether.

24 They both agree that the best way for Russ to start his presentation is

A to encourage the audience to talk.
B to explain what Russ intends to do.
C to provide an example.

25 What does the tutor advise Russ to do next while preparing his presentation?

A summarise the main point he wants to make
B read the notes he has already made
C list the topics he wants to cover

Questions 26–30

What comments does the speaker make about each of the following aspects of Russ's previous presentation?

*Choose **FIVE** answers from the box and write the correct letter, **A–G**, next to Questions 26–30.*

Comments

A lacked a conclusion
B useful in the future
C not enough
D sometimes distracting
E showed originality
F covered a wide range
G not too technical

Aspects of Russ's previous presentation

26 structure ....
27 eye contact ....
28 body language ....
29 choice of words ....
30 handouts ....

SECTION 4 *Questions 31–40*

Complete the notes below.

*Write **ONE WORD ONLY** for each answer.*

Episodic memory

- the ability to recall details, e.g. the time and **31** ……………… of past events
- different to semantic memory – the ability to remember general information about the **32** ……………… , which does not involve recalling **33** ……………… information

Forming episodic memories involves three steps:

Encoding

- involves receiving and processing information
- the more **34** ……………… given to an event, the more successfully it can be encoded
- to remember a **35** ……………… , it is useful to have a strategy for encoding such information

Consolidation

- how memories are strengthened and stored
- most effective when memories can be added to a **36** ……………… of related information
- the **37** ……………… of retrieval affects the strength of memories

Retrieval

- memory retrieval often depends on using a prompt, e.g. the **38** ……………… of an object near to the place where you left your car

Episodic memory impairments

- these affect people with a wide range of medical conditions
- games which stimulate the **39** ……………… have been found to help people with schizophrenia
- children with autism may have difficulty forming episodic memories – possibly because their concept of the **40** ……………… may be absent
- memory training may help autistic children develop social skills

READING

SECTION 1 *Questions 1–14*

Read the text below and answer Questions 1–7.

Online roommate finder: Toronto

I have one room available in a large apartment located just off Queen and Bathurst in Toronto. The room is fully furnished with a double bed, desk, shelf and wardrobe.

About us: I'm Sasha! I'm Canadian, and I've been living in this apartment since I was a teenager. I'm 23 and work in a restaurant. These past two years, my best friend has been living here but as she's now moving to Europe there is a room available as of October 1. The third room is occupied by Simon, who is from Australia. He works part-time in a music shop downtown and is a great drummer. We both like keeping the place neat and tidy – I actually enjoy cleaning in my spare time and sometimes we do it together as a roommate team (we make it fun!). I love watching movies, exploring, getting out of the city and into the outdoors, and listening to music.

The apartment itself is very large and comes equipped with unlimited wi-fi, a fully stocked kitchen, cable television, and Netflix. The bedroom is a long way from the living room, so it shouldn't disturb you if people come round and besides, we are certainly very respectful. Oh! We also have two cats who are well-behaved but they might be a problem if you have allergies. If you have a pet, that's no problem – these cats get along with other animals.

We love having people coming from other countries as it's really fun having the opportunity to show them around the neighborhood (it's a great neighborhood – lots of character and plenty to do). That said, we're certainly interested in living with Canadians too! We're very easy-going and open-minded and just hope that our new roommate will be the same.

Questions 1–7

Do the following statements agree with the information given in the text on page 37?

In boxes 1–7 on your answer sheet, write

TRUE	*if the statement agrees with the information*
FALSE	*if the statement contradicts the information*
NOT GIVEN	*if there is no information on this*

1 The room available has two beds.

2 The Australian in Sasha's apartment is a musician.

3 Sasha does all the cleaning in the apartment.

4 Sasha likes being in the open air.

5 The room available would be suitable for someone who likes to be quiet.

6 Sasha thinks her apartment is in the best part of Toronto.

7 Sasha has never had a roommate from Canada.

Read the text below and answer Questions 8–14.

Smartphone fitness apps

A Pacer

Although they were previously split into 'pro' and 'free' versions, Pacer's developer now generously includes all the features in one free app. That means you can spend no money, yet use your smartphone's GPS capabilities to track your jogging routes, and examine details of your pace and calories burned.

B Beat2

There are a wealth of running apps available, but Beat2 is a good one. This free app monitors your pace – or if you have a wrist or chest-based heart rate monitor, your beats per minute – and offers up its specially curated playlists to give you the perfect music for the pace you're running at, adding a whole new dimension to your run. The best bit is when you explode into a sprint and the music pounds in your ears. Or if you fancy something different, the app also has In-App Purchases, including tales of past sporting heroes you can listen to while you run.

C Impel

If you're serious about the sport you do, then you should be serious about Impel. As smartphone fitness tools go it's one of the best, allowing you to track your performance, set goals and see daily progress updates. If you're ever not sure where to run or cycle you can find user-created routes on the app, or share your own. All of that comes free of charge, while a premium version adds even more tools.

D Fast Track

There are plenty of GPS running apps for smartphones, but Fast Track is an excellent freebie. Although you naturally get more features if you pay for the 'pro' version, the free release gets you GPS tracking, a nicely designed map view, your training history, music, and cheering. Yes, you read the last of those right – you can have friends cheer you on as you huff and puff during a run. If you can afford the 'pro' version, you can add possible routes, voice coaches, smartwatch connectivity and more; but as a starting point, the free app gets you moving.

Questions 8–14

Look at the four reviews of smartphone fitness apps, ***A–D****, on page 39.*

For which app are the following statements true?

Write the correct letter, ***A–D****, in boxes 8–14 on your answer sheet.*

NB *You may use any letter more than once.*

8 This app can be used for more than one sport.

9 You have to pay if you want this app to suggest where you can go.

10 This app has well-presented visuals.

11 You do not have to pay for any of the features on this app.

12 You can pay to download true stories on this app.

13 You can get ideas about where to go from other people on this app.

14 This app gives you details of the energy you have used.

SECTION 2 *Questions 15–27*

Read the text below and answer Questions 15–20.

Why you should delegate tasks to team members

Delegation helps you get more done, helps your team members progress through learning new things and spreads the load in the team.

When you give someone a project task to do, make sure that they have all the information they require to actually get on and do it. That includes specifying the date it is due, writing a clear definition of the task, providing any resources they need to get it done or names of people you expect them to talk to. It also means informing them of any expectations you have, such as delivering it as a spreadsheet rather than a Word document.

If you have concerns that someone doesn't have the skills to do a good job (or they tell you this outright), make sure that you offer some help. It might take longer this time but next time they will be able to do it without you, so it will save you time in the long run.

Once you have given the task to someone, let them get on with it. Tell them how you expect to be kept informed, like through a report once a week. Then let them get on with it, unless you feel things are not progressing as you would like.

As a project manager, you have to retain some of the main project responsibilities for yourself. You shouldn't expect someone else on the project team to do your job. Equally, don't delegate tasks such as dull administrative ones, just because you don't want to do them. But remember that project management is a leadership position so you don't want your role to be seen as too basic.

One way to free up your time to spend on the more strategic and leadership parts of project management is to delegate things that are regular, like noting whether weekly targets have been met. Could someone in your team take this on for you? This can be a useful way of upskilling your team members to complement any ongoing training and allowing them to gain confidence too.

So in summary, be clear, supportive, and don't micromanage. Don't become the problem on your project that prevents progress just because you're afraid to leave people alone to get on with their jobs.

Questions 15–20

Complete the sentences below.

Choose **ONE WORD ONLY** *from the text for each answer.*

Write your answers in boxes 15–20 on your answer sheet.

15 Ensure team members are aware of any .... there are regarding how the work should be presented.

16 Make sure support is made available if any .... exist as to the team member's ability to do the work.

17 Ask the team member to detail how the work is developing, for example by providing a regular ....

18 Don't delegate administrative tasks simply because they are ....

19 Managers can ask a team member to check on the achievement of .... at fixed intervals.

20 If you .... , you risk delaying the whole project.

Read the text below and answer Questions 21–27.

Choosing the right format for your CV

A good CV should be clear, simple and easy to understand. Here are four of the most popular CV formats and advice on when to use them:

Chronological

This is the traditional CV format and is extremely popular because it allows employers to see all the posts you have held in order. It provides flexibility because it works in almost all circumstances, the exception being if you have blocks of unemployment that are difficult to account for. This type of format is particularly useful when you have a solid and complete working history spanning five years or more.

Functional

The functional CV is designed to describe your key skills rather than the jobs you have done. The functional CV format is typically used by people who have extensive gaps in their employment history, or have often changed jobs. It also suits those who want to go in a different direction work-wise and change industry. You might choose it if you want to highlight skills learned early in your career, points that might get missed if a chronological format is used. It is also appropriate if you have done little or no actual work, for example, if you are one of the current year's graduates.

Because this format is often used to cover a patchy employment history, some interviewers may view such CVs with suspicion, so be very careful should you choose it.

Achievement

An alternative to the functional CV is to use an achievement-based résumé highlighting key achievements in place of skills. This can help show your suitability for a role if you lack direct experience of it.

Non-traditional

With the explosion of digital and creative industries over recent years, CV formats have become more and more imaginative. You can present information through graphics, which can be more visually engaging and turn out to be an unusual but winning option. This will definitely make you stand out from the crowd. It also demonstrates design skills and creativity in a way that a potential employer can see and feel. However, a highly creative CV format is only really appropriate for creative and artistic sectors, such as those involving promoting products, though it would also work for the media too.

Questions 21–27

Complete the notes below.

Choose ***ONE WORD ONLY*** *from the text for each answer.*

Write your answers in boxes 21–27 on your answer sheet.

CV formats

There are several different formats including:

Chronological

- very common
- gives **21** .... in most cases
- perhaps inappropriate if there are periods where **22** .... is not easy to explain

Functional

- appropriate for people who intend to follow a new **23** .... in their career
- suits recent graduates
- can create **24** .... in recruiters, so is best used with caution

Achievement

- focuses mainly on what the person has achieved
- may be advisable if the person has no **25** .... in the area

Non-traditional

- enables use of attractive **26** .... to present data
- suits applications for jobs in marketing or **27** ....

SECTION 3 *Questions 28–40*

Read the text below and answer Questions 28–40.

DINOSAURS AND THE SECRETS THEY STILL HOLD

Dinosaur expert Dr Steve Brusatte continues to investigate the mysteries surrounding these fascinating prehistoric creatures

I was recently part of a team of palaeontologists that discovered a new dinosaur. Living in what is now China, the species would have resembled a strange bird. It was about the size of a sheep and covered in feathers, with a sharp beak that it probably used to crack open shellfish. It was given the formal scientific name *Tongtianlong*, but we called it 'Mud Dragon' because its skeleton was discovered in rock that had hardened from ancient mud. It seems that the creature got trapped in the mud and died. Then its fossil remains were found a few months ago when workmen were excavating a site in order to build a school.

It is every dinosaur-obsessed child's dearest wish to discover and name a completely new species. In fact what my colleagues and I did wasn't that unusual. New dinosaurs are appearing everywhere these days – about 50 each year. And this pace shows no signs of slowing, as different areas continue to open up to fossil hunters and a fresh generation of scientists comes of age. Because of this plentiful supply of new fossils, we now know more about dinosaurs than we do about many modern animals. But there are still many unsolved mysteries.

Dinosaurs didn't start out as huge monsters like *Tyrannosaurus Rex*. Instead they evolved from a group of angular, cat-sized reptiles called dinosauromorphs. These creatures remained small and rare for millions of years until they developed into dinosaurs. The boundary between dinosauromorphs and dinosaurs is becoming less and less distinct with each new discovery that's made, but what's becoming clear is that it took millions of years for these first dinosaurs to spread around the world, grow to huge sizes and become truly dominant.

Some discoveries in the 1970s, like the agile and strangely bird-like *Deinonychus*, proved that dinosaurs were far more dynamic and intelligent than previously thought. Some palaeontologists even proposed that they were warm-blooded creatures like modern birds with a constant high body temperature that they controlled internally, rather than from warming themselves by lying in the sun. A few decades later opinions are still mixed. The problem is that dinosaurs can't be observed. Palaeontologists must rely on studying fossils. Some results are convincing: we know from studying their bones that dinosaurs had rapid growth rates, just like modern, warm-blooded animals. Other palaeontologists, however, use the same fossils to suggest that dinosaurs were somewhere between cold-blooded reptiles and warm-blooded birds. More studies are needed to provide more clarity.

The discovery of *Deinonychus* with its long arms, skinny legs, arched neck and big claws on its feet, helped to strengthen the theory that birds evolved from dinosaurs. In the late 1990s, the discovery of thousands of feather-covered dinosaurs closed the argument. But the fossils raised another question: why did feathers first develop in dinosaurs? They probably originated as simple, hair-like strands – a necessary means of keeping warm. Many dinosaurs retained this basic fluffy coat, but in one group the strands modified. They grew bigger, started to branch out and changed into feathers like those on modern birds. They lined the arms, and sometimes the legs, forming wings. These feathers were probably for display: to attract mates or scare off rivals. They appeared in species such as the ostrich-like *Ornithomimosaur*. Such creatures were too large to fly. Flight may actually have come about by accident when smaller winged dinosaurs began jumping between trees or leaping in the air, and suddenly found that their wings had aerodynamic properties. This is one of the most stimulating new notions about dinosaurs and a fascinating area for further investigation.

There's something else that these feathers can tell us. They allow us to determine what colour dinosaurs were. If you look at modern bird feathers under a microscope, you can see tiny blobs called melanosomes. These structures contain melanin, one of the main colour-producing pigments in animals. Some are round, others are egg-shaped, etc. And that's important, because different shapes contain different colour pigments. So if you can identify the shape, you can identify the colour. A few years ago, some palaeontologists realised that you could find melanosomes in particularly well-preserved fossil feathers. They discovered that different dinosaurs had different melanosomes, which meant they had a variety of colours. Dinosaurs, therefore, probably came in a rainbow of colours – yet another thing that links them to modern birds.

The most enduring mystery of all, which has been argued about ever since the first dinosaur fossils were found, is 'Why aren't dinosaurs around today?' Of course, we now know that birds evolved from dinosaurs, so some dinosaurs do continue in a sense. But there's nothing like a *Tyrannosaurus Rex* today. They dominated the planet for over 150 million years, but suddenly disappeared from the fossil record 66 million years ago. That's when a 10 km-wide asteroid came out of space and struck what is now Mexico, impacting with huge force and unleashing earthquakes, tidal waves, wildfires and hurricane-force winds. Although palaeontologists still like to argue about what part the asteroid played in the dinosaurs' extinction, there really isn't much of a mystery left. The asteroid did it and did it quickly. There are few signs that dinosaurs were struggling before the impact. None survived except a few birds and some small furry mammals. They found themselves in an empty world, and as the planet started to recover, they evolved into new creatures, including the first apes, and so the long journey began to the beginning of humankind.

Questions 28–32

Complete the summary below.

Choose ***ONE WORD ONLY*** *from the text for each answer.*

Write your answers in boxes 28–32 on your answer sheet.

The discovery of *Tongtianlong*

This species of dinosaur has only recently been found in an area of China. Scientists believe that it was bird-like in appearance and probably no bigger than a **28** ………………………… . It is thought to have eaten **29** ………………………… and it used its **30** ………………………… to get through their hard exterior. The fossil of *Tongtianlong* was found surrounded by **31** ………………………… under the ground where the foundations of a new **32** ………………………… were being dug.

Questions 33–37

Choose the correct letter, ***A, B, C*** *or* ***D****.*

Write the correct letter in boxes 33–37 on your answer sheet.

33 What does the writer suggest about finding new dinosaurs?

A Many scientists dream of being able to do so one day.
B It is probable that most have now been discovered.
C People are running out of places to look for them.
D It is becoming relatively common to dig one up.

34 In the fourth paragraph, what does the writer suggest about palaeontologists?

A They should study the fossilised bones of dinosaurs more closely.
B Their theories are based on evidence that can be interpreted in different ways.
C It is impossible to have any confidence in the proposals they have made.
D It is worrying that they still cannot agree about dinosaurs' body temperature.

35 When describing the theory of how dinosaurs began to fly, the writer is

A amused that their flight probably came about by chance.
B surprised by the reason for the initial development of feathers.
C excited by the different possibilities it holds for future research.
D confused that feathers were also present on some creatures' legs.

36 One significance of melanosomes is that they

A provide further evidence of where birds evolved from.
B are only found in certain parts of the world.
C can be clearly seen in most fossilised feathers.
D are only found in certain birds and dinosaurs.

37 Which of the following best summarises the writer's point in the final paragraph?

A Scientists are right to continue questioning the effects of the asteroid strike.
B Large flightless dinosaurs may have existed after the asteroid hit.
C The dinosaurs were already declining before the asteroid hit.
D The effects of the asteroid strike killed most dinosaurs.

Questions 38–40

Look at the following statements (Questions 38–40) and the list of prehistoric animals below.

Match each statement with the correct animal, ***A, B, C*** *or* ***D****.*

Write the correct letter, ***A, B, C*** *or* ***D****, in boxes 38–40 on your answer sheet.*

NB *You may use any letter more than once.*

38 It may have used its feathers to frighten off members of the same species.

39 This species resembles a large flightless bird that exists today.

40 Finding this species made scientists revise their opinion of the brain power of dinosaurs.

List of Prehistoric Animals

A *Tongtianlong*

B *Tyrannosaurus Rex*

C *Deinonychus*

D *Ornithomimosaur*

WRITING

WRITING TASK 1

You should spend about 20 minutes on this task.

You recently organised an all-day meeting for your company, which took place in a local hotel. In their feedback, participants at the meeting said that they liked the hotel, but they were unhappy about the food that was served for lunch.

Write a letter to the manager of the hotel. In your letter

- ***say what the participants liked about the hotel***
- ***explain why they were unhappy about the food***
- ***suggest what the manager should do to improve the food in future***

Write at least 150 words.

You do **NOT** need to write any addresses.

Begin your letter as follows:

Dear Sir or Madam,

WRITING TASK 2

You should spend about 40 minutes on this task.

Write about the following topic:

Many working people get little or no exercise either during the working day or in their free time, and have health problems as a result.

Why do many working people not get enough exercise?

What can be done about this problem?

Give reasons for your answer and include any relevant examples from your own knowledge or experience.

Write at least 250 words.

SPEAKING

PART 1

The examiner asks the candidate about him/herself, his/her home, work or studies and other familiar topics.

EXAMPLE

Age

- Are you happy to be the age you are now? [Why/Why not?]
- When you were a child, did you think a lot about your future? [Why/Why not?]
- Do you think you have changed as you have got older? [Why/Why not?]
- What will be different about your life in the future? [Why]

PART 2

Describe a time when you started using a new technological device (e.g. a new computer or phone). **You should say:** **what device you started using** **why you started using this device** **how easy or difficult it was to use** **and explain how helpful this device was to you.**	You will have to talk about the topic for one to two minutes. You have one minute to think about what you are going to say. You can make some notes to help you if you wish.

PART 3

Discussion topics:

Technology and education

Example questions:
What is the best age for children to start computer lessons?
Do you think that schools should use more technology to help children learn?
Do you agree or disagree that computers will replace teachers one day?

Technology and society

Example questions:
How much has technology improved how we communicate with each other?
Do you agree that there are still many more major technological innovations to be made?
Could you suggest some reasons why some people are deciding to reduce their use of technology?

Test 3

LISTENING

SECTION 1 *Questions 1–10*

Complete the notes below.

*Write **ONE WORD AND/OR A NUMBER** for each answer.*

Moving to Banford City

Example

Linda recommends living in suburb of: ....*Dalton*........

Accommodation

- Average rent: **1** £ .... a month

Transport

- Linda travels to work by **2** ....
- Limited **3** .... in city centre
- Trains to London every **4** .... minutes
- Poor train service at **5** ....

Advantages of living in Banford

- New **6** .... opened recently
- **7** .... has excellent reputation
- Good **8** .... on Bridge Street

Meet Linda

- Meet Linda on **9** .... after 5.30 pm
- In the **10** .... opposite the station

SECTION 2 *Questions 11–20*

Questions 11–16

What advantage does the speaker mention for each of the following physical activities?

*Choose **SIX** answers from the box and write the correct letter, **A–G**, next to Questions 11–16.*

Advantages

A not dependent on season
B enjoyable
C low risk of injury
D fitness level unimportant
E sociable
F fast results
G motivating

Physical activities

11 using a gym ....
12 running ....
13 swimming ....
14 cycling ....
15 doing yoga ....
16 training with a personal trainer ....

Questions 17 and 18

*Choose **TWO** letters, **A–E**.*

For which **TWO** reasons does the speaker say people give up going to the gym?

A lack of time
B loss of confidence
C too much effort required
D high costs
E feeling less successful than others

Questions 19 and 20

*Choose **TWO** letters, **A–E**.*

Which **TWO** pieces of advice does the speaker give for setting goals?

A write goals down
B have achievable aims
C set a time limit
D give yourself rewards
E challenge yourself

SECTION 3 *Questions 21–30*

Questions 21–24

Choose the correct letter, ***A, B*** *or* ***C.***

Project on using natural dyes to colour fabrics

21 What first inspired Jim to choose this project?

A textiles displayed in an exhibition
B a book about a botanic garden
C carpets he saw on holiday

22 Jim eventually decided to do a practical investigation which involved

A using a range of dyes with different fibres.
B applying different dyes to one type of fibre.
C testing one dye and a range of fibres.

23 When doing his experiments, Jim was surprised by

A how much natural material was needed to make the dye.
B the fact that dyes were widely available on the internet.
C the time that he had to leave the fabric in the dye.

24 What problem did Jim have with using tartrazine as a fabric dye?

A It caused a slight allergic reaction.
B It was not a permanent dye on cotton.
C It was ineffective when used on nylon.

Questions 25–30

What problem is identified with each of the following natural dyes?

*Choose **SIX** answers from the box and write the correct letter, **A–H**, next to Questions 25–30.*

Problems

A It is expensive.
B The colour is too strong.
C The colour is not long-lasting.
D It is very poisonous.
E It can damage the fabric.
F The colour may be unexpected.
G It is unsuitable for some fabrics.
H It is not generally available.

Natural dyes

25 turmeric ....
26 beetroot ....
27 Tyrian purple ....
28 logwood ....
29 cochineal ....
30 metal oxide ....

SECTION 4 *Questions 31–40*

Complete the notes below.

Write **ONE WORD ONLY** *for each answer.*

The sleepy lizard (*tiliqua rugosa*)

Description

- They are common in Western and South Australia
- They are brown, but recognisable by their blue **31** ....
- They are relatively large
- Their diet consists mainly of **32** ....
- Their main predators are large birds and **33** ....

Navigation study

- One study found that lizards can use the **34** .... to help them navigate

Observations in the wild

- Observations show that these lizards keep the same **35** .... for several years

What people want

- Possible reasons:
  - to improve the survival of their young (but little **36** .... has been noted between parents and children)
  - to provide **37** .... for female lizards

Tracking study

- A study was carried out using GPS systems attached to the **38** .... of the lizards
- This provided information on the lizards' location and even the number of **39** .... taken
- It appeared that the lizards were trying to avoid one another
- This may be in order to reduce chances of **40** ....

SECTION 1 *Questions 1–14*

Read the text below and answer Questions 1–7.

New York Late-Starters String Orchestra

NYLSO, the New York Late-Starters String Orchestra, is something special. It was founded in early 2007, and grew out of a concept developed by The East London Late Starters Orchestra (ELLSO), an award-winning group in England. NYLSO is an amateur orchestra for adult players of violin, viola, cello, and double bass. If you played a string instrument when you were younger and would like to start again, or if you are learning as an adult and would like the chance to play in a group of similar people, then NYLSO is for you! Our goal is to create a fun, supportive, non-competitive environment for adults 18 to 80+ who wish to participate in collective music-making.

Participants should have basic music reading skills and a willingness to commit to the group, but are not required to audition. It is recommended that you have studied your instrument for at least one year. If you have ever been paid to play your instrument, recently graduated with a degree in performance, or have been playing continuously since elementary school, you may decide we are not the appropriate group for you.

How We Work:

We know that New Yorkers are busy people. It is fine if you miss an entire rehearsal period when an emergency arises. Ultimately, though, too many absences disrupt the function of the group and make it difficult to perform the pieces. Sessions are in six-week rehearsal cycles, with two-hour rehearsals held once a week. We work with the goal of producing one to three very informal 'friends-and-family' concerts per year.

Our professional tutor/facilitator serves as coach and conductor during rehearsals. Substitute conductors also join in to teach different sections, providing groups of players with valuable experience in working with different approaches and styles. Everyone is encouraged to play to their fullest potential, whatever that may be, but please recognize that while we do have a conductor, her role is not to provide one-on-one instruction during rehearsals.

NYLSO is a self-supporting collective; we do not receive any other funding. The cost is $80 for each six-week cycle. Payments are applied to the costs of rehearsal space, conductor's fees, and photocopying music.

Materials You Will Need At Rehearsals:

You will need an instrument, a portable music stand, and any other relevant accessories. You should bring a folder to keep your music together and a soft-lead pencil with an eraser for writing in changes. Sheet music is provided.

Questions 1–7

Do the following statements agree with the information given in the text on page 59?

In boxes 1–7 on your answer sheet, write

TRUE	*if the statement agrees with the information*
FALSE	*if the statement contradicts the information*
NOT GIVEN	*if there is no information on this*

1 The idea behind NYLSO was based on another orchestra.

2 An ability to read music is essential.

3 The NYLSO might be unsuitable for very advanced level musicians.

4 NYLSO concerts are free to members' families and friends.

5 Rehearsals always involve the full orchestra playing together.

6 The conductor provides her services free to NYLSO.

7 The NYLSO gives advice on what instrument to purchase.

Read the advertisements below and answer Questions 8–14.

The 7 best running watches

Kate Hilpern advises people on the best watches to use when they go running.

A Soleus FIT 1.0

Soleus claims this has everything you need and nothing you don't. Water-resistant to 30m and with a built-in rechargeable battery, it's accurate at measuring speed, pace, distance and calories burnt.

B Nike+ SportWatch GPS

You'll be hard pushed to find a running watch that finds a GPS signal quicker than this. It will keep you updated on current location, distance covered, number of laps and calories burnt.

C Garmin Forerunner

This watch, which is small enough to wear at the office, is touchscreen and is packed with impressive features, although the battery life is limited.

D Timex Run Trainer 2.0

The hi-res screen makes this a great watch for athletes at any level. The easy-to-use, upgraded menu system makes monitoring pace, speed and distance child's play. Alerts remind you when it's time to hydrate or top up the nutrition.

E Garmin Forerunner 10

This is a well-priced, entry-level watch that's light as well as waterproof and available in a range of colours. Don't expect added extras, but do expect good basic functionality.

F Nike Fuelband

Described by the Huffington Post as 'the sports watch you never knew you needed,' this soft-touch and lightweight watch has been lovingly designed to appear more like a piece of futuristic jewellery than a running watch. But it's hi-tech too and synchronises with your phone to show the results.

G Suunto Ambit2 S HR

This is better suited to off-roaders rather than urban runners and although it's quite big, it has a functional design and is compatible with the thousands of Suunto apps available.

Questions 8–14

Look at the seven advertisements for running watches, ***A–G****, on page 61.*

For which running watch are the following statements true?

Write the correct letter, ***A–G****, in boxes 8–14 on your answer sheet.*

NB *You may use any letter more than once.*

8 This would be a suitable and not too expensive first watch for a runner.

9 Care has been taken to make this watch very attractive to look at.

10 This watch can be programmed to let the runner know when it is time to get some refreshment.

11 This watch will need recharging at frequent intervals.

12 Both experienced and inexperienced runners will find this watch useful.

13 Runners will find all the features on this watch are useful.

14 People who do most of their running in cities may find this watch is not appropriate for them.

SECTION 2 *Questions 15–27*

Read the text below and answer Questions 15–22.

Employees' health and safety responsibilities

As an employee you have rights and you have responsibilities for your own wellbeing and that of your colleagues. This article explains what these responsibilities are, and how you can meet them.

Your rights

Your rights as an employee to work in a safe and healthy environment are set down in law and generally can't be changed or removed by your employer. The most important of these rights are:

- as far as possible, to have any hazards to your health and safety properly controlled
- to be given any personal protective and safety equipment without being charged for it
- to stop work and leave your work area, without being disciplined, if you have reasonable concerns about your safety
- to tell your employer about any health and safety concerns you have
- not to be disciplined if you contact the Health and Safety Executive, or your local authority, if your employer won't listen to you
- to have breaks during the time you are at work
- to have time off from work during the working week
- to have annual paid holiday.

Your responsibilities

Your most important responsibilities as an employee are:

- to take reasonable care of your own health and safety
- to remove jewellery and avoid loose clothing when operating machinery
- if you have long hair, or wear a headscarf, make sure it's tucked out of the way as it could get caught in machinery
- to take reasonable care not to expose fellow employees and members of the public to risk by what you do or don't do in the course of your work
- to co-operate with your employer, making sure you complete the training that is provided and that you understand and follow the company's health and safety policies
- not to interfere with or misuse anything that's been provided for your health, safety or welfare
- to report any injuries you suffer as a result of doing your job – your employer may then need to change the way you work.

If you drive or operate machinery, you have a responsibility to tell your employer if you take medication that makes you feel sleepy. If you do, they should temporarily move you to another job if they have one for you to do.

Questions 15–22

Complete the notes below.

Choose **ONE WORD ONLY** *from the text for each answer.*

Write your answers in boxes 15–22 on your answer sheet.

Health and Safety at Work

Employees' rights

- are established by **15** .... and include the following:
  - employers should manage any potential dangers to their staff's health and safety
  - any **16** .... needed for employees to work safely should be free
  - employees may inform management of any **17** .... they have relating to health and safety
  - employees are entitled to some **18** .... while they are working

Employees' responsibilities

- to take off jewellery and dress appropriately for their particular work
- to avoid putting colleagues and others at **19** ....
- to do any **20** .... that the employer offers
- to inform the employer of any **21** .... received while working
- to make sure the employer knows of any **22** .... you are taking that might affect performance

Read the text below and answer Questions 23–27.

Our company notices

A Advance warning

Refurbishment of offices in the Perkins Building will start on Monday 22 May, and is expected to be completed by the end of June. Staff based in that building will be individually notified of where they'll work for that time. On the previous Friday, facilities staff will move everything that needs to go to your new office. Before then, please make a list of what should be moved, and another list of what can be stored.

B Information about financial systems

The review of the company's financial systems is now complete, and modifications will shortly be introduced. Jane Phillips from Finance will explain the changes and how they affect you, and answer any queries about them, between 12 and 1 pm on 15 March in Room 5.

C Purchasing Manager

As you probably know, Sadia Ahmed is leaving the company on 31 March, after ten years as Purchasing Manager. Her replacement, Jeff Bridges, will join us on the previous Monday. Jeff will be in Room 70 between 12 and 2 pm on 3 April: feel free to drop in and say hello to him during your lunch break.

D We're doing well!

We've received a large and urgent order from one of our major customers. As a result, we'll need to run the production line for an additional three hours each evening throughout the week beginning 13 March. Any production workers willing to do this shift in addition to their normal work should speak to the Production Manager asap.

E Quality control

Because of recent concerns about product quality, we're setting up a team to consider ways of raising quality and making recommendations for changes. As staff from any department might have useful ideas, anyone is welcome to join the team – ring Rodrigo Pérez on 1012. It will involve fortnightly meetings and some research, over a six-month period.

F New opportunity

Dev Patel will cease to be part-time content editor of the company intranet at the end of April, as his new role in Marketing leaves him no time for it. We're looking for two people to take over. If you're interested, and can work an extra three or four hours a week (for extra pay, of course!), contact Maggie Campbell on 2146.

G And finally …

We hope to re-start the company tennis championship, which hasn't taken place for the last three years. If this is something for you, talk to Bill Sinclair on extension 2371. You don't need to be a star player!

Questions 23–27

*Look at the seven notices for a company's staff, **A–G**, on page 65.*

For which company notice are the following statements true?

*Write the correct letter, **A–G**, in boxes 23–27 on your answer sheet.*

23 Staff are needed to work on internal communications.

24 People are needed to help improve an internal system.

25 Staff are asked if they want to take part in an internal competition.

26 Volunteers are asked to work overtime for a limited period.

27 Staff will be told where to work temporarily.

SECTION 3 *Questions 28–40*

Read the text below and answer Questions 28–40.

Vanilla – the most wonderful flavor in the world

Vanilla is the most popular and widely used flavor in the world. And, yet, the vanilla orchid is only grown in a few countries. Below you'll discover why these countries are ideal and how the vanilla from each region differs.

Mexico

Vanilla (*Vanilla planifolia* Andrews) originated in Mexico and for centuries was the exclusive secret of the native Totonac Indians, who were later conquered by the Aztecs. The Aztecs in turn were conquered by the Spanish forces led by Cortez in 1520. He brought vanilla pods home to Spain, thus introducing the flavorful pods to the rest of the world.

However, Mexico remained the sole grower of vanilla for another 300 years. The particular relationship between the vanilla orchid and an indigenous bee called the Melipone was crucial. It was responsible for pollinating the flowers, resulting in fruit production.

Vanilla pods should be picked when the tip begins to turn yellow. The curing process gives the pods their characteristic brown color as well as their flavor and aroma. In Mexico, farmers cure the pods by wrapping them in blankets and straw mats and then placing them in ovens for 24 to 48 hours. After that, the pods are spread outdoors to absorb heat during the day and then placed in wooden boxes overnight. Once properly cured, they are stored to further develop the flavor. The entire curing process takes three to six months, making it a very labor-intensive process.

Vanilla from Mexico has a flavor that combines creamy tones with a deep, spicy character, making it a delicious complement to chocolate, cinnamon and other warm spices. It also works wonderfully in tomato sauces.

Madagascar

Around 1793, a vanilla plant was smuggled from Mexico to the Island of Réunion, east of Africa. For almost 50 years, the production of vanilla struggled. The vines grew successfully with beautiful blossoms but vanilla pods were infrequent. Without the Melipone bee, the flowers weren't being fertilized beyond occasional pollination by other insects. It wasn't until 1836 that Charles Morren, a Belgian botanist, discovered the pollination link between bee and plant. And then in 1841, Edmond Albius of Réunion developed an efficient method for fertilizing the flower by hand. Now, growers could choose the best flowers to pollinate, resulting in a healthier and higher quality vanilla pod.

Eventually, the plants arrived on the nearby island of Madagascar, where hand pollination proved its worth. Assisted by the climate and rich soil, hand pollination by the country's skilled farmers has enabled Madagascar to become the world's top vanilla producer in quantity and, many would argue, quality.

The curing process is similar to that in Mexico with one difference. The farmers initiate the process by immersing the green vanilla pods in hot water for some time. They then store them in sweat boxes before beginning the routine of spreading them outdoors during the day and packing them away at night. The different curing method used contributes to the overall flavor of the vanilla.

The sweet, creamy and mellow flavor is the one most people identify with vanilla. This flavor and the pod's ability to hold that flavor in both hot and cold applications make it an exceptional 'all-purpose' vanilla which is many people's first choice for a wide range of sweet recipes – from cooking and baking to ice creams and buttercreams.

Tahiti

Like the other countries, Tahiti's tropical climate makes it ideal for growing vanilla. However, Tahiti differs in the species of vanilla that is most common: *Vanilla tahitensis* Moore. This is the hybrid of two vanilla species introduced in the 1800s. These two species were skilfully crossed in the next few decades, to create the plump Tahitian vanilla pods we know today.

The curing process also differs from other countries'. Mature pods are first stacked in a cool place until they are completely brown (five to ten days) and then rinsed briefly in clear water, a unique characteristic of the method used in Tahiti. For the next month, growers expose the pods to the gentle morning sunlight. In the afternoon, they bind the pods in cloths and store them in crates until the next morning, to promote transpiration. Little by little, the vanilla pods lose weight and shrink. Throughout this phase, the workers carefully smooth and even out the pods with their fingers. Then after a month, the final step is to leave the pods in a shaded and well-ventilated spot for 40 days to lower their moisture content.

This species of orchid combined with Tahiti's advantageous climate and soil results in a vanilla that has fruity and sweet tones. Tahitian vanilla is especially vulnerable to heat and is therefore best used in refrigerated and frozen desserts, fruit pies and smoothies.

Indonesia

Indonesia is the second largest producer of vanilla. However, Indonesian production methods focus on quantity over quality. Unlike other regions, where vanilla beans are picked only when ripe, Indonesian growers harvest all the beans at one time, a labor-saving adjustment.

The curing process also features production shortcuts such as the use of propane heaters to speed up drying. The use of such heat, which chemically alters the beans, essentially 'burns off' flavor components while adding a smoky tone, resulting in a less complex taste and a sharper flavor. Indonesian vanilla works well when blended with vanillas from other regions and, because it's more economical, it makes the end product more affordable.

Questions 28–31

Look at the following statements (Questions 28–31) and the list of countries below.

*Match each statement with the correct country, **A**, **B**, **C** or **D**.*

*Write the correct letter, **A**, **B**, **C** or **D**, in boxes 28–31 on your answer sheet.*

28 The vanilla that is grown here was created from more than one type of vanilla plant.

29 This vanilla is often mixed with other types of vanilla.

30 Some people claim that this country produces the finest vanilla.

31 This vanilla goes well with both sweet and savoury ingredients.

List of Countries

A Mexico

B Madagascar

C Tahiti

D Indonesia

Questions 32–34

Choose the correct letter, ***A****,* ***B****,* ***C*** *or* ***D****.*

Write the correct letter in boxes 32–34 on your answer sheet.

32 What prevented countries, apart from Mexico, from growing vanilla in the 17th and 18th centuries?

A the Aztecs' refusal to let the pods be exported
B the lack of the most suitable pollinating insect
C the widespread ignorance of the existence of the plant
D the poor condition of the vanilla pods that Cortez collected

33 What does the writer suggest was the main reason for the success of vanilla cultivation on Madagascar?

A the adoption of a particular agricultural technique
B the type of vanilla orchid that was selected
C the unique quality of the soil on the island
D the rapidly increasing number of growers

34 The writer believes that Madagascan vanilla is so popular because

A it works well in a variety of main courses and puddings.
B its pod is less likely than others to break up when it is cooked.
C its taste is widely considered to be the standard taste of vanilla.
D it is the one that is used in a number of commercial frozen desserts.

Questions 35–40

Complete the summary below.

Choose ***ONE WORD ONLY*** *from the text for each answer.*

Write your answers in boxes 35–40 on your answer sheet.

How vanilla pods are cured in Tahiti

Tahitian farmers start by leaving the pods to turn **35** .... all over. They then wash them quickly before the main stage of the curing process begins. They place the pods in the **36** .... during the early part of the day. Cloths are then wrapped round them and they are left in boxes overnight. This procedure encourages **37** .... Gradually, the **38** .... of the individual pods starts to decrease. While this is happening, the farmers continue to work on the pods. They use their **39** .... to flatten them out. For the last stage in the curing process, the pods are kept in a cool place which is open to the air, so that the amount of **40** .... within them is reduced.

WRITING

WRITING TASK 1

You should spend about 20 minutes on this task.

The system used for rubbish/garbage collection in your local area is not working properly. This is causing problems for you and your neighbours.

Write a letter to the local council. In your letter

- ***describe how the rubbish collection system is not working properly***
- ***explain how this is affecting you and your neighbours***
- ***suggest what should be done about the problem***

Write at least 150 words.

You do **NOT** need to write any addresses.

Begin your letter as follows:

Dear Sir or Madam,

WRITING TASK 2

You should spend about 40 minutes on this task.

Write about the following topic:

Some people say that now we can see films on our phones or tablets there is no need to go to the cinema. Others say that to be fully enjoyed, films need to be seen in a cinema.

Discuss both these views and give your own opinion.

Give reasons for your answer and include any relevant examples from your own knowledge or experience.

Write at least 250 words.

SPEAKING

PART 1

The examiner asks the candidate about him/herself, his/her home, work or studies and other familiar topics.

EXAMPLE

Money

- When you go shopping, do you prefer to pay for things in cash or by card? [Why?]
- Do you ever save money to buy special things? [Why/Why not?]
- Would you ever take a job which had low pay? [Why/Why not?]
- Would winning a lot of money make a big difference to your life? [Why/Why not?]

PART 2

Describe an interesting discussion you had as part of your work or studies.

You should say:
what the subject of the discussion was
who you discussed the subject with
what opinions were expressed
and explain why you found the discussion interesting.

You will have to talk about the topic for one to two minutes. You have one minute to think about what you are going to say. You can make some notes to help you if you wish.

PART 3

Discussion topics:

Discussing problems with others

Example questions:
Why is it good to discuss problems with other people?
Do you think that it's better to talk to friends and not family about problems?
Is it always a good idea to tell lots of people about a problem?

Communication skills at work

Example questions:
Which communication skills are most important when taking part in meetings with colleagues?
What are the possible effects of poor written communication skills at work?
What do you think will be the future impact of technology on communication in the workplace?

Test 4

LISTENING

SECTION 1 *Questions 1–10*

Complete the notes below.

Write ***ONE WORD AND/OR A NUMBER*** *for each answer.*

Alex's Training

Example

Alex completed his training in ......*2014*......

About the applicant:

- At first, Alex did his training in the **1** .... department.
- Alex didn't have a qualification from school in **2** ....
- Alex thinks he should have done the diploma in **3** .... skills.
- Age of other trainees: the youngest was **4** ....

Benefits of doing training at JPNW:

- Lots of opportunities because of the size of the organisation.
- Trainees receive the same amount of **5** .... as permanent staff.
- The training experience increases people's confidence a lot.
- Trainees go to **6** .... one day per month.
- The company is in a convenient **7** ....

Advice for interview:

- Don't wear **8** ....
- Don't be **9** ....
- Make sure you **10** ....

SECTION 2 *Questions 11–20*

Questions 11–16

Choose the correct letter, ***A*****,** ***B*** *or* ***C*****.**

The Snow Centre

11 Annie recommends that when cross-country skiing, the visitors should

A get away from the regular trails.
B stop to enjoy views of the scenery.
C go at a slow speed at the beginning.

12 What does Annie tell the group about this afternoon's dog-sled trip?

A Those who want to can take part in a race.
B Anyone has the chance to drive a team of dogs.
C One group member will be chosen to lead the trail.

13 What does Annie say about the team relay event?

A All participants receive a medal.
B The course is 4 km long.
C Each team is led by a teacher.

14 On the snow-shoe trip, the visitors will

A visit an old gold mine.
B learn about unusual flowers.
C climb to the top of a mountain.

15 The cost of accommodation in the mountain hut includes

A a supply of drinking water.
B transport of visitors' luggage.
C cooked meals.

16 If there is a storm while the visitors are in the hut, they should

A contact the bus driver.
B wait until the weather improves.
C use the emergency locator beacon.

Questions 17–20

What information does Annie give about skiing on each of the following mountain trails?

*Choose **FOUR** answers from the box and write the correct letter, **A–F**, next to Questions 17–20.*

Information

A	It has a good place to stop and rest.
B	It is suitable for all abilities.
C	It involves crossing a river.
D	It demands a lot of skill.
E	It may be closed in bad weather.
F	It has some very narrow sections.

Mountain trails

17 Highland Trail ....

18 Pine Trail ....

19 Stony Trail ....

20 Loser's Trail ....

SECTION 3 Questions 21–30

Questions 21–26

Choose the correct letter, ***A, B*** *or* ***C***.

Labels giving nutritional information on food packaging

21 What was Jack's attitude to nutritional food labels before this project?

- **A** He didn't read everything on them.
- **B** He didn't think they were important.
- **C** He thought they were too complicated.

22 Alice says that before doing this project,

- **A** she was unaware of what certain foods contained.
- **B** she was too lazy to read food labels.
- **C** she was only interested in the number of calories.

23 When discussing supermarket brands of pizza, Jack agrees with Alice that

- **A** the list of ingredients is shocking.
- **B** he will hesitate before buying pizza again.
- **C** the nutritional label is misleading.

24 Jack prefers the daily value system to other labelling systems because it is

- **A** more accessible.
- **B** more logical.
- **C** more comprehensive.

25 What surprised both students about one flavour of crisps?

- **A** The percentage of artificial additives given was incorrect.
- **B** The products did not contain any meat.
- **C** The labels did not list all the ingredients.

26 What do the students think about research into the impact of nutritional food labelling?

- **A** It did not produce clear results.
- **B** It focused on the wrong people.
- **C** It made unrealistic recommendations.

Questions 27 and 28

*Choose **TWO** letters, **A–E**.*

Which **TWO** things surprised the students about the traffic-light system for nutritional labels?

A its widespread use
B the fact that it is voluntary for supermarkets
C how little research was done before its introduction
D its unpopularity with food manufacturers
E the way that certain colours are used

Questions 29 and 30

*Choose **TWO** letters, **A–E**.*

Which **TWO** things are true about the participants in the study on the traffic-light system?

A They had low literacy levels.
B They were regular consumers of packaged food.
C They were selected randomly.
D They were from all socio-economic groups.
E They were interviewed face-to-face.

SECTION 4 *Questions 31–40*

Complete the notes below.

Write ***ONE WORD ONLY*** *for each answer.*

The history of coffee

Coffee in the Arab world

- There was small-scale trade in wild coffee from Ethiopia.
- 1522: Coffee was approved in the Ottoman court as a type of medicine.
- 1623: In Constantinople, the ruler ordered the **31** .... of every coffee house.

Coffee arrives in Europe (17th century)

- Coffee shops were compared to **32** ....
- They played an important part in social and **33** .... changes.

Coffee and European colonisation

- European powers established coffee plantations in their colonies.
- Types of coffee were often named according to the **34** .... they came from.
- In Brazil and the Caribbean, most cultivation depended on **35** ....
- In Java, coffee was used as a form of **36** ....
- Coffee became almost as important as **37**.................................. .
- The move towards the consumption of **38** .... in Britain did not also take place in the USA.

Coffee in the 19th century

- Prices dropped because of improvements in **39** ....
- Industrial workers found coffee helped them to work at **40** ....

READING

SECTION 1 *Questions 1–14*

Read the text below and answer Questions 1–8.

The Guardian Newspaper's Travel Photography Competition

The photo competition is back, giving you another chance to win an incredible trip to Swedish Lapland.

Do you have a camera and love travelling? If so, our annual photography competition run by the Travel section of *The Guardian* is for you. It's an opportunity for you to capture the essence of the journeys you make, whether far afield or close to home, and for us to showcase your work online. The winner of each month's competition will also see their shot mounted and displayed in the end-of-year exhibition for the public at *The Guardian's* offices in London. Once the exhibition is finished, each monthly winner will receive a framed copy of their shot to place with pride on their own wall.

There will be a different theme for each month. Members of *The Guardian* travel writing team, and photographer Michael Ryan of Fotovue.com will judge the monthly entries and the overall winner.

To enter you must be living in the UK from the time you submit your entry into the competition to the time you are selected as a winner. The competition is open to all photographers (both amateur and professional).

The overall winner (chosen from the 12 monthly winners) will go on an amazing four-night trip to Swedish Lapland. The host for this specialist holiday is Fredrik Broman, who has been a nature photographer for 21 years. Fredrik will assist the winner and other participants in photographing a wide variety of winter subjects. Each day has a specific focus. The trip includes winter light photography workshops, an image editing workshop, a night photography course, and an action photography workshop.

Included in the prize: return flights from the UK, four nights' accommodation with full board, cold weather clothing for the duration of the trip – thermal overalls, winter boots, gloves, hats and woollen socks – fully qualified wilderness guides, and instructors.

The overall winner will be required to write a report of the trip, and take accompanying photographs, which will be printed in the Travel section of *The Guardian* at a later date. *The Guardian* reserves the right, however, to modify your report and photos as necessary. Your name will of course appear with the article and photos.

Questions 1–8

Do the following statements agree with the information given in the text on page 81?

In boxes 1–8 on your answer sheet, write

TRUE	*if the statement agrees with the information*
FALSE	*if the statement contradicts the information*
NOT GIVEN	*if there is no information on this*

1 This is the first year that *The Guardian* has run a travel photography competition.

2 Any photograph for the competition must have been taken on an overseas trip.

3 The end-of-year exhibition in London is free for the public to attend.

4 The judging panel is made up of a group of journalists and a professional photographer.

5 The trip to Swedish Lapland will only be offered to one winner.

6 Every activity on the trip is focused on improving photography techniques.

7 Anyone going on the trip may take some of the cold weather clothing home at the end of the trip.

8 Articles written about the trip may be changed before being published.

Read the text below and answer Questions 9–14.

Running headphones

Listening to music on headphones makes running and even working out at the gym much more enjoyable. Here are some alternatives to choose from.

A Plantronics Backbeat Fit

These headphones are really tough so you don't need to worry about just throwing them into your bag before or after a workout. As well as providing reasonably clear sound they will also last a remarkable eight hours on a single charge.

B Sennheiser CX685 Sports

These headphones are impressively practical. Designed to fit firmly in your ear, however energetic you are, they're tight without being uncomfortable, and have a handy remote and a mic for phone calls. They will also resist some water being spilt on them.

C Nokia WH-510 Coloud Pop

These stylish headphones have fantastic bass, giving you a bit of extra oomph when you run. They also have a tangle-free cable which avoids any time-consuming messing about before you set off on your run.

D Sony NWZ-W273S

It's hard to imagine using any other headphones once you've tried these. As well as being wireless and waterproof at a depth of 2m, they even have a built-in MP3 player that can hold up to 1,000 songs. A charge provides up to an hour of playback.

E Betron B750S

If you're on a tight budget, it can always feel risky buying a bottom of the market pair of headphones, but with these you needn't worry. Not only do they provide fair sound quality, they also come with a pouch to keep them in.

F Happy Plugs

The sound quality on these is decent, although you're probably not going to be hugely impressed. They also come with a handy remote built into the cable to skip and pause songs with while you work out.

G Powerbeats 2

If money is not an issue, then these are definitely worth considering. They make everything sound so crisp and they're so light and comfortable that it's easy to forget that you're even wearing them.

Questions 9–14

Look at the seven reviews of headphones, ***A–G****, on page 83.*

For which headphones are the following statements true?

Write the correct letter, ***A–G****, in boxes 9–14 on your answer sheet.*

NB *You may use any letter more than once.*

9 These headphones would suit someone who doesn't mind spending a lot to get good quality.

10 The battery on these headphones has a surprisingly long life.

11 It is possible to keep in contact with other people while using these headphones.

12 Although these headphones are cheaper than most, music sounds quite good through them.

13 These headphones are very strong and do not require gentle handling.

14 These headphones allow users to move around their playlist of music easily while they are exercising.

SECTION 2 *Questions 15–27*

Read the text below and answer Questions 15–21.

A case study of a risk assessment for general office cleaning

A commercial cleaning service took on a new contract to clean an office complex. Before sending cleaning staff to the offices, the manager of the cleaning service carried out a risk assessment using guidance provided by the Health and Safety Executive (HSE).

To identify the hazards, the cleaning service manager visited the office complex and walked through the areas where cleaning staff would be working, noting things that might pose potential risks. Following this, he consulted the health and safety representatives of the cleaning service about these risks, taking into account the needs of any particular staff members, such as whether they were pregnant or aged under 18.

In order to gather further information, he then had a meeting with the client company during which a number of issues were discussed. These included the client company's own standard of housekeeping, such as the immediate clearing up of spills and keeping walkways clear, as well as the action to be taken if a fire broke out. He also established what facilities and equipment would be available to the cleaners, including the amount of storage space available, as well as the availability of sinks and taps, etc. and agreed on a method of reporting near-miss accidents and risks discovered by cleaners (e.g. damaged floor tiles).

Following the meeting, the manager created a risk assessment document. He wrote down who could be harmed by each risk or hazard identified and in what way, and he then described what controls, if any, were in existence to manage these hazards. The manager then compared these to the good practice guidance set out on the HSE's website and identified any areas where improvement was needed.

The manager discussed the findings with the cleaning staff, making sure they understood the risks of the job and how these risks would be monitored. One cleaner, whose first language was not English, had difficulty understanding this, so the manager arranged for translation to be done by a bilingual cleaner from another team. Finally, to ensure that all the cleaning staff had access to a copy of the risk assessment, the manager pinned a copy in the cupboard where cleaning equipment was kept.

Questions 15–21

Complete the flow-chart below.

*Choose **ONE WORD ONLY** from the text for each answer.*

Write your answers in boxes 15–21 on your answer sheet.

Stages followed by manager in carrying out risk assessment

He visited the offices to be cleaned and noted potential risks.

▼

He talked to health and safety **15** .... about the risks.

▼

At a meeting, he talked to the client company about

- the policy of the company regarding **16** .... (e.g. clear walkways)
- procedures to be followed in case of a **17** ....
- facilities available to cleaners (e.g. space available for **18** ....)
- a way of **19** .... risks and hazards.

▼

He created a risk assessment document identifying existing controls of risks and hazards.

▼

He compared these to information that the HSE provided on its **20** ....

▼

He displayed a copy of the risk assessment inside a

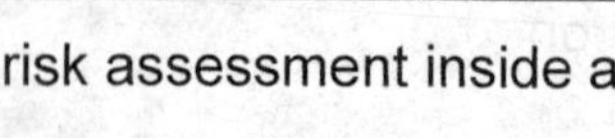

21 .... available to all cleaning staff.

Read the text below and answer Questions 22–27.

Preparing for a virtual job interview

Businesses are always looking for new ways to increase efficiency and profits. For example, organisations often reduce costs by conducting virtual job interviews. The video or Skype interview benefits both interviewer and interviewee, especially when an applicant would otherwise need to travel far. Despite the convenience though, it poses unique challenges.

How a virtual interview is the same

The typical interview process usually entails multiple steps. First, there is screening, lasting about thirty minutes. Its purpose is to ensure candidates have the basic requirements. In the second interview, they're assessed for their technical skills and on whether they would fit the organisation.

Virtual interviews follow the same steps so you'll need to focus on the same core topics. Identify what the critical topics are based on the job description and prepare to talk about them. If you can, gather inside information so you can impress interviewers with your knowledge.

How a virtual interview is different

Normally, you travel somewhere for an interview. One advantage of that is that you aren't responsible for the place, whereas in a virtual interview you must ensure you have an appropriate location and appropriate equipment.

Modern technology is great when it works, but a pain when it doesn't. So, it's wise to check you can operate your webcam, especially if you don't use it often. Test the headset too and find out how intelligible your voice sounds. It's also wise to establish what software the interviewer is going to work with and give it a trial run.

Probably the biggest problem in a virtual interview is what the camera can see. You want the interviewer to see you as a professional. Having a messy or cluttered room behind you won't help you achieve this image – a clear white background is usually a safe bet.

The most important part of your preparation is to run through everything first as best you can. Have a friend conduct a rehearsal with you before the big day. This will help you know how to behave in front of the camera.

All things considered, though, virtual interviews should be treated like any other type of interview. Being at home requires as much preparation as a traditional interview. If you follow the steps mentioned above, you have every chance of getting the job you want. Good luck!

Questions 22–27

Complete the sentences below.

Choose **ONE WORD ONLY** *from the text for each answer.*

Write your answers in boxes 22–27 on your answer sheet.

22 Some companies prefer to interview job applicants digitally because of lower ....

23 As with the standard recruitment process, virtual recruitment opens with ....

24 Applicants should read any details about the advertised post carefully and pick out important .... which they can discuss if necessary.

25 It is a good idea for applicants to check if they can be clearly understood when they use a ....

26 Applicants may not be familiar with the .... that the person conducting the interview will use, so they should try it out.

27 It is very useful to go through a .... of the interview, with someone playing the part of the interviewer.

SECTION 3 *Questions 28–40*

Read the text below and answer Questions 28–40.

Tuning up your leadership skills

Does jazz music offer lessons for today's leaders?

A Ever since management expert Peter Drucker compared the job of Chief Executive Officer to that of an orchestra conductor, the business world has been exploring comparisons and inspirations from the world of music. Now Warwick Business School Professors Deniz Ucbasaran and Andy Lockett are hitting all the right notes with their study of famous jazz musicians, *Leading Entrepreneurial Teams: Insights From Jazz*, providing some essential insights for entrepreneurial team leaders.

Ucbasaran and Lockett (together with Durham Business School Professor Michael Humphries) chose jazz for a number of reasons. For a start, jazz bands are synonymous with creativity, improvisation and innovation, all essential ingredients for entrepreneurship. Jazz groups and their members often operate in uncertain and dynamic environments, characterised by rapid change. Yet through collective endeavour many jazz bands find their own structure and harmony and become profitable enterprises – both creatively and commercially.

B The authors decided to focus on three of the best known names in jazz – Duke Ellington, Miles Davis and Art Blakey. American composer Duke Ellington was a pioneering jazz orchestra leader from the 1920s through to the 1970s. Trumpet player Miles Davis was instrumental in the development of a number of new jazz styles, including bebop and jazz fusion. Jazz drummer Arthur 'Art' Blakey became famous as the leader of his band the *Jazz Messengers*.

The research focused on the way that these jazz greats created and ran their musical enterprises. In particular, Ucbasaran and Lockett focused on three specific areas of leadership activity: team formation, team coordination and team turnover.

There were strong similarities in the processes the band leaders used to assemble their diverse teams of talent. In particular, they looked for musicians with a different sound or way of playing, one that was unique to that band member and would improve the overall sound of the band. That feature was as much bound up with the personality of the individual musician as it was to do with their technical proficiency.

C But disparate teams, many different personalities, and high levels of creativity are a recipe for group conflict. And, sure enough, there was plenty of dysfunctional conflict and disruptive clashes of egos and personalities evident in the jazz ensembles. Traditional team leadership theory suggests that to get the best team performance the leader should foster conflict that is productive in its effects, while minimising destructive conflict. But this is difficult when the sources of productive and destructive conflict are the same; that is, differences in personality and thinking. So how do leaders deal with destructive conflict? It didn't seem to bother the likes of Ellington, Davis and Blakey. Their attitude was 'the music comes first'. The moments of musical genius when everything came together excused minor problems such as if individuals occasionally turned up late for practice, or stepped out of a performance for a quick snack.

D Teams must coordinate their behaviour and action to achieve an outcome. The team leader can assume a number of different roles when helping the team achieve its objectives. Some leaders are very directive, detailing what tasks they want team members to perform, and how they want them to go about those tasks.

But that was not the approach Ellington, Davis and Blakey adopted. Instead, these leaders acted more as facilitators, empowering the musicians to collectively coordinate their behaviour and action to produce the desired outcome. As Ucbasaran and Lockett note, Miles Davis discouraged band members from rehearsing in case it led to musical clichés from over-practice. Similarly, he often asked his musicians to play a piece in an unusual key, so they did not rely on learned fingering patterns. The performers were not left entirely to their own devices though. All three leaders created a general framework within which team members could work, providing guidance but also the freedom to explore, express and make mistakes.

E The third aspect of leadership behaviour that Ucbasaran and her colleagues looked at was managing team turnover – people joining and leaving the team. In the jazz ensembles studied, musicians joined and left on a regular basis. Yet the high turnover of team members, despite the resulting loss of knowledge and skills, was seen in a positive light. That was partly because of the advantages of getting a fresh shot of knowledge, ideas and creativity when new members joined.

A common reason for the jazz musicians leaving was that they felt sufficiently qualified to go and run another band. The three band leaders were understanding about this, particularly as it was a process they had also been through. In some cases, in particular with Art Blakey, they actively encouraged and coached team members to become leaders. As the jazz icons Ellington, Davis and Blakey would no doubt agree, there is no magic score that if followed note by note will make you a great leader of creative talent. However, take an entrepreneur, a few cues from the aforementioned jazz trio, mix in a little improvisation, and you are more likely to hear the sweet sound of success. As Louis Armstrong once sang: 'Now that's jazz'.

Questions 28–33

The text on pages 89 and 90 has five sections, **A–E**.

Which section contains the following?

Write the correct letter, ***A–E****, in boxes 28–33 on your answer sheet.*

NB *You may choose any letter more than once.*

28 a summary of the different aspects of leadership that are covered in the study

29 a description of how band leaders sometimes passed on their leadership skills to others

30 a summary of the backgrounds of the band leaders chosen for the study

31 examples of ways in which one band leader encouraged his musicians to be more creative

32 an overview of the main similarities between the work of business people and jazz musicians

33 a description of two contrasting ways of leading a team

Questions 34–36

Do the following statements agree with the information given in the text on pages 89 and 90?

In boxes 34–36 on your answer sheet, write

TRUE *if the statement agrees with the information*
FALSE *if the statement contradicts the information*
NOT GIVEN *if there is no information on this*

34 The study by Ucbasaran and Lockett was the first to compare the worlds of music and business.

35 One reason why jazz musicians were chosen for the research is because the setting in which they work is unpredictable.

36 The researchers decided to cover only certain aspects of leadership.

Questions 37–40

*Choose the correct letter, **A**, **B**, **C** or **D**.*

Write the correct letter in boxes 37–40 on your answer sheet.

37 When assembling their teams, the band leaders all prioritised players

- **A** who had special technical skill.
- **B** who were used to working independently.
- **C** who had an individual style of their own.
- **D** who would get on well with other band members.

38 What obstacle might jazz leaders face in reducing destructive conflict among team members?

- **A** They may also reduce productive conflict in the process.
- **B** Their team members tend to have especially strong personalities.
- **C** They are unaware of the theory concerning different types of conflict.
- **D** Their team members may be unwilling to cooperate in reducing this.

39 What approach to group coordination was shared by Ellington, Davis and Blakey?

- **A** They allowed musicians to be creative within certain agreed limits.
- **B** They increased opportunities for success and reduced chances of failure.
- **C** They provided a structure within which musicians could express themselves.
- **D** They coordinated the work of their teams so each member contributed equally.

40 Ucbasaran and her colleagues found that the high turnover of members in jazz bands

- **A** was eventually reduced by the policies of the band leaders.
- **B** was welcomed by band leaders for the benefits it brought.
- **C** was due to a shortage of effective band leaders.
- **D** was a feature of the growing popularity of jazz.

WRITING

WRITING TASK 1

You should spend about 20 minutes on this task.

A friend you made while you were studying abroad has written to ask you for help in finding a job in your country. You have heard about a job in a local company that might be suitable for him/her.

Write a letter to this friend. In your letter

- ***tell your friend about the job and what sort of work it involves***
- ***say why you think the job would be suitable for him/her***
- ***explain how to apply for the job***

Write at least 150 words.

You do **NOT** need to write any addresses.

Begin your letter as follows:

Dear ....,

WRITING TASK 2

You should spend about 40 minutes on this task.

Write about the following topic:

Some people say it is important to keep your home and your workplace tidy, with everything organised and in the correct place.

What is your opinion about this?

Give reasons for your answer and include any relevant examples from your own knowledge or experience.

Write at least 250 words.

SPEAKING

PART 1

The examiner asks the candidate about him/herself, his/her home, work or studies and other familiar topics.

EXAMPLE

Animals

- Are there many animals or birds where you live? [Why/Why not?]
- How often do you watch programmes or read articles about wild animals? [Why?]
- Have you ever been to a zoo or a wildlife park? [Why/Why not?]
- Would you like to have a job working with animals? [Why/Why not?]

PART 2

Describe a website you use that helps you a lot in your work or studies.

You should say:
what the website is
how often you use the website
what information the website gives you
and explain how your work or studies would change if this website didn't exist.

You will have to talk about the topic for one to two minutes. You have one minute to think about what you are going to say. You can make some notes to help you if you wish.

PART 3

Discussion topics:

The internet

Example questions:
Why do some people find the internet addictive?
What would the world be like without the internet?
Do you think that the way people use the internet may change in the future?

Social media websites

Example questions:
What are the ways that social media can be used for positive purposes?
Why do some individuals post highly negative comments about other people on social media?
Do you think that companies' main form of advertising will be via social media in the future?

Audioscripts

TEST 1

SECTION 1

OFFICIAL: Hello, Tourist Information Centre, Mike speaking, how can I help you?

WOMAN: Oh, hi. I wanted to find out about cookery classes. I believe there are some one-day classes for tourists?

OFFICIAL: Well, they're open to everyone, but tourists are always welcome. OK, let me give you some details of what's available. There are several classes. One very popular one is at the Food Studio. *Example*

WOMAN: OK.

OFFICIAL: They focus on seasonal products, and as well as teaching you how to cook them, they also show you how to choose them. *Q1*

WOMAN: Right, that sounds good. How big are the classes?

OFFICIAL: I'm not sure exactly, but they'll be quite small.

WOMAN: And could I get a private lesson there? *Q2*

OFFICIAL: I think so … let me check, yes, they do offer those. Though in fact most of the people who attend the classes find it's a nice way of getting to know one another.

WOMAN: I suppose it must be, yes.

OFFICIAL: And this company has a special deal for clients where they offer a discount of 20 percent if you return for a further class. *Q3*

WOMAN: OK. But you said there were several classes?

OFFICIAL: That's right. Another one you might be interested in is Bond's Cookery School. They're quite new, they just opened six months ago, but I've heard good things about them. They concentrate on teaching you to prepare healthy food, and they have quite a lot of specialist staff. *Q4*

WOMAN: So is that food for people on a diet and things like that? I don't know if I'd be interested in that.

OFFICIAL: Well, I don't think they particularly focus on low calorie diets or weight loss. It's more to do with recipes that look at specific needs, like including ingredients that will help build up your bones and make them stronger, that sort of thing. *Q5*

WOMAN: I see. Well, I might be interested, I'm not sure. Do they have a website I could check?

OFFICIAL: Yes, just key in the name of the school – it'll come up. And if you want to know more about them, every Thursday evening they have a lecture at the school. It's free and you don't need to book or anything, just turn up at 7.30. And that might give you an idea of whether you want to go to an actual class. *Q6*

OFFICIAL: OK, there's one more place you might be interested in. That's got a rather strange name, it's called The Arretsa Centre – that's spelled A-R-R-E-T-S-A. *Q7*

WOMAN: OK.

OFFICIAL: They've got a very good reputation. They do a bit of meat and fish cookery but they mostly specialise in vegetarian dishes. *Q8*

WOMAN: Right. That's certainly an area I'd like to learn more about. I've got lots of friends who don't eat meat. In fact, I think I might have seen that school today. Is it just by the market? *Q9*

OFFICIAL: That's right. So they don't have any problem getting their ingredients. They're right next door. And they also offer a special two-hour course in how to use a knife. They cover all the different skills – buying them, sharpening, chopping techniques. It gets booked up quickly though so you'd need to check it was available. Q10

WOMAN: Right, well thank you very much. I'll go and …

SECTION 2

Good evening everyone. My name's Phil Sutton, and I'm chairman of the Highways Committee. We've called this meeting to inform members of the public about the new regulations for traffic and parking we're proposing for Granford. I'll start by summarising these changes before we open the meeting to questions.

So, why do we need to make these changes to traffic systems in Granford? Well, we're very aware that traffic is becoming an increasing problem. It's been especially noticeable with the increase in heavy traffic while they've been building the new hospital. But it's the overall rise in the volume of traffic of all kinds that's concerning us. To date there's not been any increase in traffic accidents, but that's not something we want to see happen, obviously. Q11

We recently carried out a survey of local residents, and their responses were interesting. People were very concerned about the lack of visibility on some roads due to cars parked along the sides of the roads. We'd expected complaints about the congestion near the school when parents are dropping off their children or picking them up, but this wasn't top of the list, and nor were noise and fumes from trucks and lorries, though they were mentioned by some people. Q12

We think these new traffic regulations would make a lot of difference. But we still have a long way to go. We've managed to keep our proposals within budget, just, so they can be covered by the Council. But, of course, it's no good introducing new regulations if we don't have a way of making sure that everyone obeys them, and that's an area we're still working on with the help of representatives from the police force. Q13

OK, so this slide shows a map of the central area of Granford, with the High Street in the middle and School Road on the right. Now, we already have a set of traffic lights in the High Street at the junction with Station Road, but we're planning to have another set at the other end, at the School Road junction, to regulate the flow of traffic along the High Street. Q14

We've decided we definitely need a pedestrian crossing. We considered putting this on School Road, just outside the school, but in the end we decided that could lead to a lot of traffic congestion, so we decided to locate it on the High Street, crossing the road in front of the supermarket. That's a very busy area, so it should help things there. Q15

We're proposing some changes to parking. At present, parking isn't allowed on the High Street outside the library, but we're going to change that, and allow parking there, but not at the other end of the High Street near School Road. Q16

There'll be a new 'No Parking' sign on School Road, just by the entrance to the school, forbidding parking for 25 metres. This should improve visibility for drivers and pedestrians, especially on the bend just to the north of the school. Q17

As far as disabled drivers are concerned, at present they have parking outside the supermarket, but lorries also use those spaces, so we've got two new disabled parking spaces on the side road up towards the bank. It's not ideal, but probably better than the present arrangement. *Q18*

We also plan to widen the pavement on School Road. We think we can manage to get an extra half-metre on the bend just before you get to the school, on the same side of the road. *Q19*

Finally, we've introduced new restrictions on loading and unloading for the supermarket, so lorries will only be allowed to stop there before 8 am. That's the supermarket on School Road – we kept to the existing arrangements with the High Street supermarket. *Q20*

OK. So that's about it. Now, would anyone ...

SECTION 3

EMMA: We've got to choose a topic for our experiment, haven't we, Jack? Were you thinking of something to do with seeds?

JACK: That's right. I thought we could look at seed germination – how a seed begins to grow.

EMMA: OK. Any particular reason? I know you're hoping to work in plant science eventually ...

JACK: Yeah, but practically everything we do is going to feed into that. No, there's an optional module on seed structure and function in the third year that I might do, so I thought it might be useful for that. If I choose that option, I don't have to do a dissertation module. *Q21*

EMMA: Good idea.

JACK: Well, I thought for this experiment we could look at the relationship between seed size and the way the seeds are planted. So, we could plant different sized seeds in different ways, and see which grow best.

EMMA: OK. We'd need to allow time for the seeds to come up. *Q22*

JACK: That should be fine if we start now. A lot of the other possible experiments need quite a bit longer.

EMMA: So that'd make it a good one to choose. And I don't suppose it'd need much equipment; we're not doing chemical analysis or anything. Though that's not really an issue, we've got plenty of equipment in the laboratory.

JACK: Yeah. We need to have a word with the tutor if we're going to go ahead with it though. I'm sure our aim's OK. It's not very ambitious but the assignment's only ten percent of our final mark, isn't it? But we need to be sure we're the only ones doing it. *Q23*

EMMA: Yeah, it's only five percent actually, but it'd be a bit boring if everyone was doing it.

JACK: Did you read that book on seed germination on our reading list?

EMMA: The one by Graves? I looked through it for my last experiment, though it wasn't all that relevant there. It would be for this experiment, though. I found it quite hard to follow – lots about the theory, which I hadn't expected. *Q24*

JACK: Yes, I'd been hoping for something more practical. It does include references to the recent findings on genetically-modified seeds, though.

EMMA: Yes, that was interesting.

JACK: I read an article about seed germination by Lee Hall.

EMMA: About seeds that lie in the ground for ages and only germinate after a fire?

JACK: That's the one. I knew a bit about it already, but not about this research. His analysis of figures comparing the times of the fires and the proportion of seeds that germinated was done in a lot of detail – very impressive. Q25

EMMA: Was that the article with the illustrations of early stages of plant development? They were very clear.

JACK: I think those diagrams were in another article.

EMMA: Anyway, shall we have a look at the procedure for our experiment? We'll need to get going with it quite soon.

JACK: Right. So the first thing we have to do is find our seeds. I think vegetable seeds would be best. And obviously they mustn't all be the same size. So, how many sorts do we need? About four different ones? Q26

EMMA: I think that would be enough. There'll be quite a large number of seeds for each one.

JACK: Then, for each seed we need to find out how much it weighs, and also measure its dimensions, and we need to keep a careful record of all that. Q27

EMMA: That'll be quite time-consuming. And we also need to decide how deep we're going to plant the seeds – right on the surface, a few millimetres down, or several centimetres. Q28

JACK: OK. So then we get planting. Do you think we can plant several seeds together in the same plant pot? Q29

EMMA: No, I think we need a different one for each seed.

JACK: Right. And we'll need to label them – we can use different coloured labels. Then we wait for the seeds to germinate – I reckon that'll be about three weeks, depending on what the weather's like. Then we see if our plants have come up, and write down how tall they've grown. Q30

EMMA: Then all we have to do is look at our numbers, and see if there's any relation between them.

JACK: That's right. So ...

SECTION 4

Hi. Today we're going to be looking at animals in urban environments and I'm going to be telling you about some research on how they're affected by these environments.

Now, in evolutionary terms, urban environments represent huge upheavals, the sorts of massive changes that usually happen over millions of years. And we used to think that only a few species could adapt to this new environment. One species which is well known as being highly adaptable is the crow, and there've been various studies about how they manage to learn new skills. Another successful species is the pigeon, because they're able to perch on ledges on the walls of city buildings, just like they once perched on cliffs by the sea. Q31 Q32

But in fact, we're now finding that these early immigrants were just the start of a more general movement of animals into cities, and of adaptation by these animals to city life. And one thing that researchers are finding especially interesting is the speed with which they're doing this – we're not talking about gradual evolution here – these animals are changing fast. Q33

Let me tell you about some of the studies that have been carried out in this area. So, in the University of Minnesota, a biologist called Emilie Snell-Rood and her colleagues looked at specimens of urbanised small mammals such as mice and gophers that had been collected in Minnesota, and that are now kept in museums there. And she looked at specimens that had been collected over the last hundred years, which is a very short time in evolutionary terms. And she found that during that time, these small mammals had experienced a jump in brain size when compared to rural mammals. Now, we can't be sure this means they're more intelligent, but since the sizes of other parts of the body didn't change, it does suggest that something cognitive was going on. And Snell-Rood thinks that this change might reflect the cognitive demands of adjusting to city life – having to look in different places to find food, for example, and coping with a whole new set of dangers. *Q34* *Q35*

Then over in Germany at the Max Planck Institute, there's another biologist called Catarina Miranda who's done some experiments with blackbirds living in urban and rural areas. And she's been looking not at their anatomy but at their behaviour. So as you might expect, she's found that the urban blackbirds tend to be quite bold – they're prepared to face up to a lot of threats that would frighten away their country counterparts. But there's one type of situation that does seem to frighten the urban blackbirds, and that's anything new – anything they haven't experienced before. And if you think about it, that's quite sensible for a bird living in the city. *Q36* *Q37*

Jonathan Atwell, in Indiana University, is looking at how a range of animals respond to urban environments. He's found that when they're under stress, their endocrine systems react by reducing the amount of hormones such as corticosterone into their blood. It's a sensible-seeming adaptation. A rat that gets scared every time a subway train rolls past won't be very successful. *Q38*

There's just one more study I'd like to mention which is by Sarah Partan and her team, and they've been looking at how squirrels communicate in an urban environment, and they've found that a routine part of their communication is carried out by waving their tails. You do also see this in the country, but it's much more prevalent in cities, possibly because it's effective in a noisy environment. *Q39*

So what are the long-term implications of this? One possibility is that we may see completely new species developing in cities. But on the other hand, it's possible that not all of these adaptations will be permanent. Once the animal's got accustomed to its new environment, it may no longer need the features it's developed. *Q40*

So, now we've had a look ...

TEST 2

SECTION 1

JIM: Hello, South City Cycling Club.

WOMAN: Oh, hi. Er ... I want to find out about joining the club.

JIM: Right. I can help you there. I'm the club secretary and my name's Jim Hunter. *Example*

WOMAN: Oh, hi Jim.

JIM: So, are you interested in membership for yourself?

WOMAN: That's right.

JIM: OK. Well there are basically two types of adult membership. If you're pretty serious about cycling, there's the Full membership. That costs 260 dollars and that covers you not just for ordinary cycling but also for races both here in the city and also in other parts of Australia. *Q1*

WOMAN: Right. Well, I'm not really up to that standard. I was more interested in just joining a group to do some cycling in my free time.

JIM: Sure. That's why most people join. So, in that case you'd be better with the Recreational membership. That's 108 dollars if you're over 19, and 95 dollars if you're under.

WOMAN: I'm 25.

JIM: OK. It's paid quarterly, and you can upgrade it later to the Full membership if you want to, of course. Now both types of membership include the club fee of 20 dollars. They also provide insurance in case you have an accident, though we hope you won't need that, of course. *Q2*

WOMAN: No. OK, well, I'll go with the Recreational membership, I think. And that allows me to join in the club activities, and so on?

JIM: That's right. And once you're a member of the club, you're also permitted to wear our kit when you're out cycling. It's green and white.

WOMAN: Yes, I've seen cyclists wearing it. So, can I buy that at the club?

JIM: No, it's made to order by a company in Brisbane. You can find them online; they're called Jerriz. That's J-E-R-R-I-Z. You can use your membership number to put in an order on their website. *Q3*

WOMAN: OK. Now, can you tell me a bit about the rides I can do?

JIM: Sure. So we have training rides pretty well every morning, and they're a really good way of improving your cycling skills as well as your general level of fitness, but they're different levels. Level A is pretty fast – you're looking at about 30 or 35 kilometres an hour. If you can do about 25 kilometres an hour, you'd probably be level B, and then level C are the novices, who stay at about 15 kilometres per hour. *Q4*

WOMAN: Right. Well I reckon I'd be level B. So, when are the sessions for that level?

JIM: There are a couple each week. They're both early morning sessions. There's one on Tuesdays, and for that one you meet at 5.30 am, and the meeting point's the stadium – do you know where that is? *Q5*

WOMAN: Yes, it's quite near my home, in fact. OK, and how about the other one?

JIM: That's on Thursdays. It starts at the same time, but they meet at the main gate to the park. *Q6*

WOMAN: Is that the one just past the shopping mall?

JIM: That's it.

WOMAN: So how long are the rides?

JIM: They're about an hour and a half. So, if you have a job it's easy to fit in before you go to work. And the members often go somewhere for coffee afterwards, so it's quite a social event. *Q7*

WOMAN: OK. That sounds good. I've only just moved to the city so I don't actually know many people yet.

JIM: Well, it's a great way to meet people.

WOMAN: And does each ride have a leader? *Q8*

JIM: Sometimes, but not always. But you don't really need one; the group members on the ride support one another, anyway.

WOMAN: How would we know where to go?

JIM: If you check the club website, you'll see that the route for each ride is clearly marked. So you can just print that out and take it along with you. It's similar from one week to another, but it's not always exactly the same. *Q9*

WOMAN: And what do I need to bring?

JIM: Well, bring a bottle of water, and your phone. You shouldn't use it while you're cycling, but have it with you.

WOMAN: Right.

JIM: And in winter, it's well before sunrise when we set out, so you need to make sure your bike's got lights. *Q10*

WOMAN: That's OK. Well, thanks Jim. I'd definitely like to join. So what's the best way of going about it?

JIM: You can …

SECTION 2

Thanks for coming everyone. OK, so this meeting is for new staff and staff who haven't been involved with our volunteering projects yet. So basically, the idea is that we allow staff to give up some of their work time to help on various charity projects to benefit the local community. We've been doing this for the last five years and it's been very successful.

Participating doesn't necessarily involve a huge time commitment. The company will pay for eight hours of your time. That can be used over one or two days all at once, or spread over several months throughout the year. There are some staff who enjoy volunteering so much they also give up their own free time for a couple of hours every week. It's completely up to you. Obviously, many people will have family commitments and aren't as available as other members of staff. *Q11*

Feedback from staff has been overwhelmingly positive. Because they felt they were doing something really useful, nearly everyone agreed that volunteering made them feel more motivated at work. They also liked building relationships with the people in the local community and felt valued by them. One or two people also said it was a good thing to have on their CVs. *Q12*

One particularly successful project last year was the Get Working Project. This was aimed at helping unemployed people in the area get back to work. Our staff were able to help them improve their telephone skills, such as writing down messages and speaking with confidence to potential customers, which they had found quite difficult. This is something many employers look for in job applicants – and something we all do without even thinking about, every day at work. *Q13*

We've got an exciting new project starting this year. Up until now, we've mainly focused on projects to do with education and training. And we'll continue with our reading project in schools and our work with local charities. But we've also agreed to help out on a conservation project in Redfern Park. So if any of you fancy being outside and getting your hands dirty, this is the project for you. Q14

I also want to mention the annual Digital Inclusion Day, which is coming up next month. The aim of this is to help older people keep up with technology. And this year, instead of hosting the event in our own training facility, we're using the ICT suite at Hill College, as it can hold far more people. Q15

We've invited over 60 people from the Silver Age Community Centre to take part, so we'll need a lot of volunteers to help with this event.

If you're interested in taking part, please go to the volunteering section of our website and complete the relevant form. We won't be providing any training for this but you'll be paired with an experienced volunteer if you've never done it before. By the way, don't forget to tell your manager about any volunteering activities you decide to do. Q16

The participants on the Digital Inclusion Day really benefited. The majority were in their seventies, though some were younger and a few were even in their nineties! Quite a few owned both a computer and a mobile phone, but these tended to be outdated models. Q17 They generally knew how to do simple things, like send texts, but weren't aware of recent developments in mobile phone technology. A few were keen to learn but most were quite dismissive at first – they couldn't see the point of updating their skills. But that soon changed. Q18

The feedback was very positive. The really encouraging thing was that participants all said they felt much more confident about using social media to keep in touch with their grandchildren, who prefer this form of communication to phoning or sending emails. A lot of them also said playing online games would help them make new friends and keep their brains active. They weren't that impressed with being able to order their groceries online, as they liked going out to the shops, but some said it would come in handy if they were ill or the weather was really bad. One thing they asked about was using tablets for things like reading newspapers – some people had been given tablets as presents but had never used them, so that's something we'll make sure we include this time … Q19 Q20

SECTION 3

TUTOR: Ah … come in, Russ.

RUSS: Thank you.

TUTOR: Now you wanted to consult me about your class presentation on nanotechnology – you're due to give it in next week, aren't you?

RUSS: That's right. And I'm really struggling. I chose the topic because I didn't know much about it and wanted to learn more, but now I've read so much about it, in a way there's too much to say – I could talk for much longer than the twenty minutes I've been allocated. Should I assume the other students don't know much, and give them a kind of general introduction, or should I try and make them share my fascination with a particular aspect? Q21

TUTOR: You could do either, but you'll need to have it clear in your own mind.

RUSS: Then I think I'll give an overview.

TUTOR: OK. Now, one way of approaching this is to work through developments in chronological order.

RUSS: Uh-huh.

TUTOR: On the other hand, you could talk about the numerous ways that nanotechnology is being applied.

RUSS: You mean things like thin films on camera displays to make them water-repellent, and additives to make motorcycle helmets stronger and lighter.

TUTOR: Exactly. Or another way would be to focus on its impact in one particular area, say medicine, or space exploration. *Q22*

RUSS: That would make it easier to focus. Perhaps I should do that.

TUTOR: I think that would be a good idea.

RUSS: Right. How important is it to include slides in the presentation?

TUTOR: They aren't essential, by any means. And there's a danger of tailoring what you say to fit whatever slides you can find. While it can be good to include slides, you could end up spending too long looking for suitable ones. You might find it better to leave them out. *Q23*

RUSS: I see. Another thing I was wondering about was how to start. I know presentations often begin with 'First I'm going to talk about this, and then I'll talk about that', but I thought about asking the audience what they know about nanotechnology.

TUTOR: That would be fine if you had an hour or two for the presentation, but you might find that you can't do anything with the answers you get, and it simply eats into the short time that's available.

RUSS: So, maybe I should mention a particular way that nanotechnology is used, to focus people's attention. *Q24*

TUTOR: That sounds sensible.

RUSS: What do you think I should do next? I really have to plan the presentation today and tomorrow.

TUTOR: Well, initially I think you should ignore all the notes you've made, take a small piece of paper, and write a single short sentence that ties together the whole presentation: it can be something as simple as 'Nanotechnology is already improving our lives'. Then start planning the content around that. You can always modify that sentence later, if you need to. *Q25*

RUSS: OK.

TUTOR: OK, now let's think about actually giving the presentation. You've only given one before, if I remember correctly, about an experiment you'd been involved in.

RUSS: That's right. It was pretty rubbish!

TUTOR: Let's say it was better in some respects than in others. With regard to the structure, I felt that you ended rather abruptly, without rounding it off. Be careful not to do that in next week's presentation. *Q26*

RUSS: OK.

TUTOR: And you made very little eye contact with the audience, because you were looking down at your notes most of the time. You need to be looking at the audience and only occasionally glancing at your notes. *Q27*

RUSS: Mmm.

TUTOR: Your body language was a little odd. Every time you showed a slide, you turned your back on the audience so you could look at it – you should have been looking at your laptop. And you kept scratching your head, so I found myself wondering when you were next going to do that, instead of listening to what you were saying! *Q28*

RUSS: Oh dear. What did you think of the language? I knew that not everyone was familiar with the subject, so I tried to make it as simple as I could.

TUTOR: Yes, that came across. You used a few words that are specific to the field, but you always explained what they meant, so the audience wouldn't have had any difficulty understanding. *Q29*

RUSS: Uh-huh.

TUTOR: I must say the handouts you prepared were well thought out. They were a good summary of your presentation, which people would be able to refer to later on. So well done on that. Q30

RUSS: Thank you.

TUTOR: Well, I hope that helps you with next week's presentation.

RUSS: Yes, it will. Thanks a lot.

TUTOR: I'll look forward to seeing a big improvement, then.

SECTION 4

Today, we'll be continuing the series of lectures on memory by focusing on what is called episodic memory and what can happen if this is not working properly.

Episodic memory refers to the memory of an event or 'episode'. Episodic memories allow us to mentally travel back in time to an event from the past. Episodic memories include various details about these events, for example, when an event happened and other information such as the location. To help understand this concept, try to remember the last time you ate dinner at a restaurant. The ability to remember where you ate, who you were with and the items you ordered are all features of an episodic memory. Q31

Episodic memory is distinct from another type of memory called semantic memory. This is the type of factual memory that we have in common with everyone else – that is your general knowledge of the world. To build upon a previous example, remembering where you parked your car is an example of episodic memory, but your understanding of what a car is and how an engine works are examples of semantic memory. Unlike episodic memory, semantic memory isn't dependent on recalling personal experiences. Q32 Q33

Episodic memory can be thought of as a process with several different steps of memory processing: encoding, consolidation and retrieval.

The initial step is called encoding. This involves the process of receiving and registering information, which is necessary for creating memories of information or events that you experience. The degree to which you can successfully encode information depends on the level of attention you give to an event while it's actually happening. Being distracted can make effective encoding very difficult. Encoding of episodic memories is also influenced by how you process the event. For example, if you were introduced to someone called Charlie, you might make the connection that your uncle has the same name. Future recollection of Charlie's name is much easier if you have a strategy to help you encode it. Q34 Q35

Memory consolidation, the next step in forming an episodic memory, is the process by which memories of encoded information are strengthened, stabilised and stored to facilitate later retrieval. Consolidation is most effective when the information being stored can be linked to an existing network of information. Consolidation makes it possible for you to store memories for later retrieval indefinitely. Forming strong memories depends on the frequency with which you try to retrieve them. Memories can fade or become harder to retrieve if they aren't used very often. Q36 Q37

The last step in forming episodic memories is called retrieval, which is the conscious recollection of encoded information. Retrieving information from episodic memory depends upon semantic, olfactory, auditory and visual factors. These help episodic memory retrieval by acting as a prompt. For example, when recalling where you parked your car you may use the colour of a sign close to where you parked. You actually have to mentally travel back to the moment you parked. Q38

There are a wide range of neurological diseases and conditions that can affect episodic memory. These range from Alzheimer's to schizophrenia to autism. An impairment of episodic memory can have a profound effect on individuals' lives. For example, the symptoms of schizophrenia can be reasonably well controlled by medication; however, patients' episodic memory may still be impaired and so they are often unable to return to university or work. Recent studies have shown that computer-assisted games designed to keep the brain active *Q39* can help improve their episodic memory.

Episodic memories can help people connect with others, for instance by sharing intimate *Q40* details about their past; something individuals with autism often have problems with. This may be caused by an absence of a sense of self. This is essential for the storage of episodic memory, and has been found to be impaired in children with autism. Research has shown that treatments that improve memory may also have a positive impact on children's social development.

One study looked at a ...

TEST 3

SECTION 1

LINDA: Hello, Linda speaking.

MATT: Oh hi, Linda. This is Matt Brooks. Alex White gave me your number. He said you'd be able to give me some advice about moving to Banford.

LINDA: Yes, Alex did mention you. How can I help?

MATT: Well, first of all – which area to live in?

LINDA: Well, I live in Dalton, which is a really nice suburb – not too expensive, and there's a nice park. *Example*

MATT: Sounds good. Do you know how much it would be to rent a two bedroom flat there?

LINDA: Yeah, you should be able to get something reasonable for 850 pounds per month. That's what people typically pay. You certainly wouldn't want to pay more than 900 pounds. That doesn't include bills or anything. *Q1*

MATT: No. That sounds alright. I'll definitely have a look there. Are the transport links easy from where you live?

LINDA: Well, I'm very lucky. I work in the city centre so I don't have to use public transport. I go by bike. *Q2*

MATT: Oh, I wish I could do that. Is it safe to cycle around the city?

LINDA: Yes, it's fine. And it keeps me fit. Anyway, driving to work in the city centre would be a nightmare because there's hardly any parking. And the traffic during the rush hour can be bad. *Q3*

MATT: I'd be working from home but I'd have to go to London one or two days a week.

LINDA: Oh, that's perfect. Getting to London is no problem. There's a fast train every 30 minutes which only takes 45 minutes. *Q4*

MATT: That's good.

LINDA: Yeah, the train service isn't bad during the week. And they run quite late at night. It's weekends that are a problem. They're always doing engineering work and you have to take a bus to Hadham and pick up the train there, which is really slow. But other than that, Banford's a great place to live. I've never been happier. *Q5*

LINDA: There are some nice restaurants in the city centre and a brand new cinema which has only been open a couple of months. There's a good arts centre too. *Q6*

MATT: Sounds like Banford's got it all.

LINDA: Yes! We're really lucky. There are lots of really good aspects to living here. The schools are good and the hospital here is one of the best in the country. Everyone I know who's been there's had a positive experience. Oh, I can give you the name of my dentist too in Bridge Street, if you're interested. I've been going to him for years and I've never had any problems. *Q7* *Q8*

MATT: Oh, OK. Thanks!

LINDA: I'll find his number and send it to you.

MATT: Thanks, that would be really helpful.

LINDA: Are you planning to visit Banford soon?

MATT: Yes. My wife and I are both coming next week. We want to make some appointments with estate agents.

LINDA: I could meet you if you like and show you around.

MATT: Are you sure? We'd really appreciate that.

LINDA: Either a Tuesday or Thursday is good for me, after 5.30. *Q9*

MATT: Thursday's preferable – Tuesday I need to get home before 6 pm.

LINDA: OK. Great. Let me know which train you're catching and I'll meet you in the café outside. You can't miss it. It's opposite the station and next to the museum. *Q10*

MATT: Brilliant. I'll text you next week then. Thanks so much for all the advice.

LINDA: No problem. I'll see you next week.

SECTION 2

So if you're one of those people who hasn't found the perfect physical activity yet – here are some things to think about which might help you make the right decision for you.

The first question to ask yourself is whether you would enjoy training in a gym. Many people are put off by the idea of having to fit a visit to the gym into their busy day – you often have to go very early or late as some gyms can get very crowded. But with regular training you'll see a big difference in a relatively short space of time. *Q11*

Running has become incredibly popular in recent years. That's probably got a lot to do with the fact that it's a very accessible form of exercise – anyone can run – even if you can only run a few metres to begin with. But make sure you get the right shoes – it's worth investing in a high quality pair and they don't come cheap. Another great thing about running is that you can do it at any time of day or night – the only thing that may stop you is snow and ice. *Q12*

Swimming is another really good way to build fitness. What attracts many people is that you can swim in an indoor pool at any time of year. On the other hand, it can be quite boring or solitary – it's hard to chat to people while you're swimming lengths. *Q13*

Cycling has become almost as popular as running in recent years. That's probably because as well as improving their fitness, many people say being out in the fresh air in a park or in the countryside can be fun, provided the conditions are right, of course – only fanatics go out in the wind and rain! *Q14*

Yoga is a good choice for those of you looking for exercise which focuses on developing both a healthy mind and body. It's a good way of building strength and with the right instructor, there's less chance of hurting yourself than with other more active sports. But don't expect to find it easy – it can be surprisingly challenging, especially for people who aren't very flexible. *Q15*

Getting a personal trainer is a good way to start your fitness programme. Obviously there can be significant costs involved. But if you've got someone there to encourage you and help you achieve your goals, you're less likely to give up. Make sure you get someone with a recognised qualification, though, or you could do yourself permanent damage. *Q16*

Whatever you do, don't join a gym unless you're sure you'll make good use of it. So many people waste lots of money by signing up for membership and then hardly ever go. What happens to their good intentions? I don't think people suddenly stop caring about improving their fitness, or decide they have more important things to do. I think people lose interest when they don't think they're making enough progress. That's when they give up hope and stop believing they'll ever achieve their goals. Also, what people sometimes don't realise when they start is that it takes a lot of determination and hard work to keep training week after week and lots of people don't have that kind of commitment. *Q17 & Q18*

One thing you can do to help yourself is to set manageable goals – be realistic and don't push yourself too far. Some people advise writing goals down, but I think it's better to have a flexible approach. Give yourself a really nice treat every time you reach one of your goals. And don't get too upset if you experience setbacks – it's a journey – there are bound to be difficulties along the way. *Q19 & Q20*

SECTION 3

TUTOR: OK, Jim. You wanted to see me about your textile design project.

JIM: That's right. I've been looking at how a range of natural dyes can be used to colour fabrics like cotton and wool.

TUTOR: Why did you choose that topic?

JIM: Well, I got a lot of useful ideas from the museum, you know, at that exhibition of textiles. But I've always been interested in anything to do with colour. Years ago, I went to a carpet shop with my parents when we were on holiday in Turkey, and I remember all the amazing colours. Q21

TUTOR: They might not all have been natural dyes.

JIM: Maybe not, but for the project I decided to follow it up. And I found a great book about a botanic garden in California that specialises in plants used for dyes.

TUTOR: OK. So, in your project, you had to include a practical investigation.

JIM: Yeah. At first I couldn't decide on my variables. I was going to just look at one type of fibre for example, like cotton ...

TUTOR: ... and see how different types of dyes affected it?

JIM: Yes. Then I decided to include others as well, so I looked at cotton and wool and nylon. Q22

TUTOR: With just one type of dye?

JIM: Various types, including some that weren't natural, for comparison.

TUTOR: OK.

JIM: So, I did the experiments last week. I used some ready-made natural dyes, I found a website which supplied them, they came in just a few days, but I also made some of my own.

TUTOR: That must have taken quite a bit of time.

JIM: Yes, I'd thought it'd just be a matter of a teaspoon or so of dye, and actually that wasn't the case at all. Like I was using one vegetable, beetroot, for a red dye, and I had to chop up a whole pile of it. So it all took longer than I'd expected. Q23

TUTOR: One possibility is to use food colourings.

JIM: I did use one. That was a yellow dye, an artificial one.

TUTOR: Tartrazine?

JIM: Yeah. I used it on cotton first. It came out a great colour, but when I rinsed the material, the colour just washed away. I'd been going to try it out on nylon, but I abandoned that idea. Q24

TUTOR: Were you worried about health issues?

JIM: I'd thought if it's a legal food colouring, it must be safe.

TUTOR: Well, it can occasionally cause allergic reactions, I believe.

TUTOR: So what natural dyes did you look at?

JIM: Well, one was turmeric. The colour's great, it's a really strong yellow. It's generally used in dishes like curry.

TUTOR: It's meant to be quite good for your health when eaten, but you might find it's not permanent when it's used as a dye – a few washes, and it's gone. Q25

JIM: Right. I used beetroot as a dye for wool. When I chop up beetroot to eat I always end up with bright red hands, but the wool ended up just a sort of watery cream shade. Disappointing. Q26

TUTOR: There's a natural dye called Tyrian purple. Have you heard of that?

JIM: Yes. It comes from a shellfish, and it was worn in ancient times but only by important people as it was so rare. I didn't use it. Q27

TUTOR: It fell out of use centuries ago, though one researcher managed to get hold of some recently. But that shade of purple can be produced by chemical dyes nowadays. Did you use any black dyes?

JIM: Logwood. That was quite complicated. I had to prepare the fabric so the dye would take.

TUTOR: I hope you were careful to wear gloves.

JIM: Yes. I know the danger with that dye.

TUTOR: Good. It can be extremely dangerous if it's ingested. Now, presumably you had a Q28
look at an insect-based dye? Like cochineal, for example?

JIM: Yes. I didn't actually make that, I didn't have time to start crushing up insects to get the red colour and anyway they're not available here, but I managed to get the dye quite easily from a website. But it cost a fortune. I can see why it's generally just Q29
used in cooking, and in small quantities.

TUTOR: Yes, it's very effective, but that's precisely why it's not used as a dye.

JIM: I also read about using metal oxide. Apparently you can allow iron to rust while it's in contact with the fabric, and that colours it.

TUTOR: Yes, that works well for dying cotton. But you have to be careful as the metal can Q30
actually affect the fabric and so you can't expect to get a lot of wear out of fabrics treated in this way. And the colours are quite subtle, not everyone likes them. Anyway, it looks as if you've done a lot of work …

SECTION 4

Last week, we started looking at reptiles, including crocodiles and snakes. Today, I'd like us to have a look at another reptile – the lizard – and in particular, at some studies that have been done on a particular type of lizard whose Latin name is *tiliqua rugosa*. This is commonly known as the sleepy lizard, because it's quite slow in its movements and spends quite a lot of its time dozing under rocks or lying in the sun.

I'll start with a general description. Sleepy lizards live in Western and South Australia, where they're quite common. Unlike European lizards, which are mostly small, green and fast-moving, sleepy lizards are brown, but what's particularly distinctive about them is the colour of Q31
their tongue, which is dark blue, in contrast with the lining of their mouth which is bright pink. And they're much bigger than most European lizards. They have quite a varied diet, including Q32
insects and even small animals, but they mostly eat plants of varying kinds.

Even though they're quite large and powerful, with strong jaws that can crush beetles and snail shells, they still have quite a few predators. Large birds like cassowaries were one of the main ones in the past, but nowadays they're more likely to be caught and killed by snakes. Actually, Q33
another threat to their survival isn't a predator at all, but is man-made – quite a large number of sleepy lizards are killed by cars when they're trying to cross highways.

One study carried out by Michael Freake at Flinders University investigated the methods of navigation of these lizards. Though they move slowly, they can travel quite long distances. And he found that even if they were taken some distance away from their home territory, they could Q34
usually find their way back home as long as they could see the sky – they didn't need any other landmarks on the ground.

Observations of these lizards in the wild have also revealed that their mating habits are quite unusual. Unlike most animals, it seems that they're relatively monogamous, returning to the Q35
same partner year after year. And the male and female also stay together for a long time, both before and after the birth of their young.

It's quite interesting to think about the possible reasons for this. It could be that it's to do with protecting their young – you'd expect them to have a much better chance of survival if they have both parents around. But in fact observers have noted that once the babies have hatched out of their eggs, <u>they have hardly any contact with their parents</u>. So, there's not really any evidence to support that idea. *Q36*

Another suggestion's based on the observation that male lizards in monogamous relationships tend to be bigger and stronger than other males. So maybe the male lizards stay around so <u>they can give the female lizards protection from other males</u>. But again, we're not really sure. *Q37*

Finally, I'd like to mention another study that involved collecting data by tracking the lizards. I was actually involved in this myself. So we caught some lizards in the wild and <u>we developed a tiny GPS system that would allow us to track them, and we fixed this onto their tails</u>. Then we set the lizards free again, and we were able to track them for twelve days and gather data, not just about their location, <u>but even about how many steps they took during this period</u>. *Q38* *Q39*

One surprising thing we discovered from this is that there were far fewer meetings between lizards than we expected – it seems that they were actually trying to avoid one another. So why would that be? Well, again we have no clear evidence, but <u>one hypothesis is that male lizards can cause quite serious injuries to one another, so maybe this avoidance is a way of preventing this</u> – of self-preservation, if you like. But we need to collect a lot more data before we can be sure of any of this. *Q40*

TEST 4

SECTION 1

MARTHA: Hi Alex. It's Martha Clines here. James White gave me your number. I hope you don't mind me calling you.

ALEX: Of course not. How are you, Martha?

MARTHA: Good thanks. I'm ringing because I need a bit of advice.

ALEX: Oh yeah. What about?

MARTHA: The training you did at JPNW a few years ago. I'm applying for the same thing.

ALEX: Oh right. Yes, I did mine in 2014. Best thing I ever did. I'm still working there. *Example*

MARTHA: Really? What are you doing?

ALEX: Well, now I work in the customer services department but I did my initial training *Q1*
in Finance. I stayed there for the first two years and then moved to where I am now.

MARTHA: That's the same department I'm applying for. Did you enjoy it?

ALEX: I was pretty nervous to begin with. I didn't do well in my exams at school and I
was really worried because I failed Maths. But it didn't actually matter because I *Q2*
did lots of courses on the job.

MARTHA: Did you get a diploma at the end of your trainee period? I'm hoping to do the one in business skills.

ALEX: Yes. That sounds good. I took the one on IT skills but I wish I'd done that *Q3*
one instead.

MARTHA: OK, that's good to know. What about the other trainees? How did you get on with them?

ALEX: There were about 20 of us who started at the same time and we were all around
the same age – I was 18 and there was only one person younger than me, who *Q4*
was 17. The rest were between 18 and 20. I made some good friends.

MARTHA: I've heard lots of good things about the training at JPNW. It seems like there are a lot of opportunities there.

ALEX: Yeah, definitely. Because of its size you can work in loads of different areas within the organisation.

MARTHA: What about pay? I know you get a lower minimum wage than regular employees.

ALEX: That's right – which isn't great. But you get the same number of days' holiday as *Q5*
everyone else. And the pay goes up massively if they offer you a job at the end of the training period.

MARTHA: Yeah, but I'm not doing it for the money – it's the experience I think will be really useful. Everyone says by the end of the year you gain so much confidence.

ALEX: You're right. That's the most useful part about it. There's a lot of variety too. You're given lots of different things to do. I enjoyed it all – I didn't even mind the studying.

MARTHA: Do you have to spend any time in college?

ALEX: Yes, one day each month. So you get lots of support from both your tutor and *Q6*
your manager.

MARTHA: That's good. And the company is easy to get to, isn't it?

ALEX: Yes, it's very close to the train station so the location's a real advantage. *Q7*

ALEX: Have you got a date for your interview yet?

MARTHA: Yes, it's on the 23rd of this month.

ALEX: So long as you're well prepared there's nothing to worry about. Everyone's very friendly.

MARTHA: I am not sure what I should wear. What do you think?

ALEX: Nothing too casual – like jeans, for example. If you've got a nice jacket, wear that with a skirt or trousers. *Q8*

MARTHA: OK. Thanks. Any other tips?

ALEX: Erm, well I know it's really obvious but arrive in plenty of time. They hate people who are late. So make sure you know exactly where you have to get to. And one other useful piece of advice my manager told me before I had the interview for this job – is to smile. Even if you feel terrified. It makes people respond better to you. *Q9* *Q10*

MARTHA: I'll have to practise doing that in the mirror!

ALEX: Yeah – well, good luck. Let me know if you need any more information.

MARTHA: Thanks very much.

SECTION 2

Hi everyone, welcome to the Snow Centre. My name's Annie. I hope you enjoyed the bus trip from the airport – we've certainly got plenty of snow today! Well, you've come to New Zealand's premier snow and ski centre, and we've a whole load of activities for you during your week here.

Most visitors come here for the cross-country skiing, where you're on fairly flat ground for most of the time, rather than going down steep mountainsides. There are marked trails, but you can also leave these and go off on your own and that's an experience not to be missed. You can go at your own speed – it's great aerobic exercise if you really push yourself, or if you prefer you can just glide gently along and enjoy the beautiful scenery. *Q11*

This afternoon, you'll be going on a dog-sled trip. You may have seen our dogs on TV recently racing in the winter sled festival. If you want, you can have your own team for the afternoon and learn how to drive them, following behind our leader on the trail. Or if you'd prefer, you can just sit back in the sled and enjoy the ride as a passenger. *Q12*

At the weekend, we have the team relay event, and you're all welcome to join in. We have a local school coming along, and a lot of the teachers are taking part too. Participation rather than winning is the main focus, and there's a medal for everyone who takes part. Participants are in teams of two to four, and each team must complete four laps of the course. *Q13*

For your final expedition, you'll head off to Mount Frenner wearing a pair of special snow shoes which allow you to walk on top of the snow. This is an area where miners once searched for gold, though there are very few traces of their work left now. When the snow melts in summer, the mountain slopes are carpeted in flowers and plants. It's a long ascent, though not too steep, and walkers generally take a couple of days to get to the summit and return. *Q14*

You'll spend the night in our hut half-way up the mountain. That's included in your package for the stay. It's got cooking facilities, firewood and water for drinking. For washing, we recommend you use melted snow, though, to conserve supplies. We can take your luggage up on our snowmobile for you for just ten dollars a person. The hut has cooking facilities so you can make a hot meal in the evening and morning, but you need to take your own food. *Q15*

The weather on Mount Frenner can be very stormy. In that case, stay in the hut – generally the storms don't last long. Don't stress about getting back here to the centre in time to catch the airport bus – they'll probably not be running anyway. We do have an emergency locator beacon in the hut but only use that if it's a real emergency, like if someone's ill or injured. *Q16*

Now, let me tell you something about the different ski trails you can follow during your stay here.

Highland Trail's directly accessible from where we are now. This trail's been designed to give first-timers an experience they'll enjoy regardless of their age or skill, but it's also ideal for experts to practise their technique. *Q17*

Then there's Pine Trail ... if you're nervous about skiing, leave this one to the experts! You follow a steep valley looking right down on the river below – scary! But if you've fully mastered the techniques needed for hills, it's great fun. *Q18*

Stony Trail's a good choice once you've got a general idea of the basics. There are one or two tricky sections, but nothing too challenging. There's a shelter half-way where you can sit and take a break and enjoy the afternoon sunshine. *Q19*

And finally, Loser's Trail. This starts off following a gentle river valley but the last part is quite exposed so the snow conditions can be challenging – if it's snowing or windy, check with us before you set out to make sure the trail's open that day. *Q20*

Right, so now if you'd like to follow me, we'll get started ...

SECTION 3

JACK: I've still got loads to do for our report on nutritional food labels.

ALICE: Me too. What did you learn from doing the project about your own shopping habits?

JACK: Well, I've always had to check labels for traces of peanuts in everything I eat because of my allergy. But beyond that I've never really been concerned enough to check how healthy a product is. *Q21*

ALICE: This project has actually taught me to read the labels much more carefully. I tended to believe claims on packaging like 'low in fat'. But I now realise that the 'healthy' yoghurt I've bought for years is full of sugar and that it's actually quite high in calories. *Q22*

JACK: Ready meals are the worst ... comparing the labels on supermarket pizzas was a real eye-opener. Did you have any idea how many calories they contain? I was amazed.

ALICE: Yes, because unless you read the label really carefully, you wouldn't know that the nutritional values given are for half a pizza. *Q23*

JACK: When most people eat the whole pizza. Not exactly transparent is it?

ALICE: Not at all. But I expect it won't stop you from buying pizza?

JACK: Probably not, no! I thought comparing the different labelling systems used by food manufacturers was interesting. I think the kind of labelling system used makes a big difference.

ALICE: Which one did you prefer?

JACK: I liked the traditional daily value system best – the one which tells you what proportion of your required daily intake of each ingredient the product contains. I'm not sure it's the easiest for people to use but at least you get the full story. I like to know all the ingredients in a product – not just how much fat, salt and sugar they contain. *Q24*

ALICE: But it's good supermarkets have been making an effort to provide reliable information for customers.

JACK: Yes. There just needs to be more consistency between labelling systems used by different supermarkets, in terms of portion sizes, etc.

ALICE: Mmm. The labels on the different brands of chicken flavour crisps were quite revealing too, weren't they?

JACK: Yeah. I don't understand how they can get away with calling them chicken flavour when they only contain artificial additives. *Q25*

ALICE: I know. I'd at least have expected them to contain a small percentage of real chicken.
JACK: Absolutely.
ALICE: I think having nutritional food labeling has been a good idea, don't you? I think it will change people's behaviour and stop mothers, in particular, buying the wrong things.
JACK: But didn't that study kind of prove the opposite? People didn't necessarily stop buying unhealthy products.
ALICE: They only said that might be the case. Those findings weren't that conclusive and it was quite a small-scale study. I think more research has to be done. *Q26*
JACK: Yes, I think you're probably right.

JACK: What do you think of the traffic-light system?
ALICE: I think supermarkets like the idea of having a colour-coded system – red, orange or green – for levels of fat, sugar and salt in a product.
JACK: But it's not been adopted universally. And not on all products. Why do you suppose that is? *Q27 & Q28*
ALICE: Pressure from the food manufacturers. Hardly surprising that some of them are opposed to flagging up how unhealthy their products are.
JACK: I'd have thought it would have been compulsory. It seems ridiculous it isn't.
ALICE: I know. And what I couldn't get over is the fact that it was brought in without enough consultation – a lot of experts had deep reservations about it.
JACK: That is a bit weird. I suppose there's an argument for doing the research now when consumers are familiar with this system.
ALICE: Yeah, maybe.
JACK: The participants in the survey were quite positive about the traffic-light system.
ALICE: Mmm. But I don't think they targeted the right people. They should have focused on people with low literacy levels because these labels are designed to be accessible to them.
JACK: Yeah. But it's good to get feedback from all socio-economic groups. And there wasn't much variation in their responses. *Q29 & Q30*
ALICE: No. But if they hadn't interviewed participants face-to-face, they could have used a much bigger sample size. I wonder why they chose that method?
JACK: Dunno. How were they selected? Did they volunteer or were they approached?
ALICE: I think they volunteered. The thing that wasn't stated was how often they bought packaged food – all we know is how frequently they used the supermarket.

SECTION 4

In my presentation, I'm going to talk about coffee, and its importance both in economic and social terms. We think it was first drunk in the Arab world, but there's hardly any documentary evidence of it before the 1500s, although of course that doesn't mean that people didn't know about it before then.

However, there is evidence that coffee was originally gathered from bushes growing wild in Ethiopia, in the northeast of Africa. In the early sixteenth century, it was being bought by traders, and gradually its use as a drink spread throughout the Middle East. It's also known that in 1522, in the Turkish city of Constantinople, which was the centre of the Ottoman Empire, the court physician approved its use as a medicine.

By the mid-1500s, coffee bushes were being cultivated in the Yemen and for the next hundred years this region produced most of the coffee drunk in Africa and the Arab world. What's particularly interesting about coffee is its effect on social life. It was rarely drunk at home, but instead people went to coffee houses to drink it. These people, usually men, would meet to drink coffee and chat about issues of the day. But at the time, this chance to share ideas and opinions was seen as something that was potentially dangerous, and in 1623 the ruler of Constantinople demanded the destruction of all the coffee houses in the city, although after his death many new ones opened, and coffee consumption continued. In the seventeenth century, coffee drinking spread to Europe, and here too coffee shops became places where ordinary people, nearly always men, could meet to exchange ideas. Because of this, some people said that these places performed a similar function to universities. The opportunity they provided for people to meet together outside their own homes and to discuss the topics of the day had an enormous impact on social life, and many social movements and political developments had their origins in coffee house discussions. *Q31* *Q32* *Q33*

In the late 1600s, the Yemeni monopoly on coffee production broke down and coffee production started to spread around the world, helped by European colonisation. Europeans set up coffee plantations in Indonesia and the Caribbean and production of coffee in the colonies skyrocketed. Different types of coffee were produced in different areas, and it's interesting that the names given to these different types, like Mocha or Java coffee, were often taken from the port they were shipped to Europe from. But if you look at the labour system in the different colonies, there were some significant differences. *Q34*

In Brazil and the various Caribbean colonies, coffee was grown in huge plantations and the workers there were almost all slaves. But this wasn't the same in all colonies; for example in Java, which had been colonised by the Dutch, the peasants grew coffee and passed a proportion of this on to the Dutch, so it was used as a means of taxation. But whatever system was used, under the European powers of the eighteenth century, coffee production was very closely linked to colonisation. Coffee was grown in ever-increasing quantities to satisfy the growing demand from Europe, and it became nearly as important as sugar production, which was grown under very similar conditions. However, coffee prices were not yet low enough for people to drink it regularly at home, so most coffee consumption still took place in public coffee houses and it still remained something of a luxury item. In Britain, however, a new drink was introduced from China, and started to become popular, gradually taking over from coffee, although at first it was so expensive that only the upper classes could afford it. This was tea, and by the late 1700s it was being widely drunk. However, when the USA gained independence from Britain in 1776, they identified this drink with Britain, and coffee remained the preferred drink in the USA, as it still is today. *Q35* *Q36* *Q37* *Q38*

So, by the early nineteenth century, coffee was already being widely produced and consumed. But during this century, production boomed and coffee prices started to fall. This was partly because new types of transportation had been developed which were cheaper and more efficient. So now, working people could afford to buy coffee – it wasn't just a drink for the middle classes. And this was at a time when large parts of Europe were starting to work in industries. And sometimes this meant their work didn't stop when it got dark; they might have to continue throughout the night. So, the use of coffee as a stimulant became important – it wasn't just a drink people drank in the morning, for breakfast. *Q39* *Q40*

There were also changes in cultivation …

Listening and Reading Answer Keys

TEST 1

LISTENING

Section 1, Questions 1–10

1 choose
2 private
3 20 / twenty percent
4 healthy
5 bones
6 lecture
7 Arretsa
8 vegetarian
9 market
10 knife

Section 2, Questions 11–20

11 B
12 C
13 B
14 E
15 D
16 B
17 G
18 C
19 H
20 I

Section 3, Questions 21–30

21 A
22 C
23 B
24 C
25 B
26 G
27 C
28 H
29 A
30 E

Section 4, Questions 31–40

31 crow
32 cliffs
33 speed
34 brain(s)
35 food
36 behaviour(s) / behavior(s)
37 new
38 stress
39 tail(s)
40 permanent

If you score …

0–16	17–25	26–40
you are unlikely to get an acceptable score under examination conditions and we recommend that you spend a lot of time improving your English before you take IELTS.	you may get an acceptable score under examination conditions but we recommend that you think about having more practice or lessons before you take IELTS.	you are likely to get an acceptable score under examination conditions but remember that different institutions will find different scores acceptable.

READING

Reading Section 1, Questions 1–14

1 B
2 F
3 D
4 E
5 A
6 E
7 G
8 FALSE
9 TRUE
10 NOT GIVEN
11 FALSE
12 TRUE
13 NOT GIVEN
14 FALSE

Reading Section 2, Questions 15–27

15 shipment
16 photo ID
17 (cab) lights
18 sleeper areas
19 immigration
20 charge
21 chair
22 allergy
23 dependants
24 flexible
25 dismissal
26 doctor
27 stress

Reading Section 3, Questions 28–40

28 ix
29 iv
30 ii
31 iii
32 vi
33 x
34 vii
35 i
36 viii
37 ocean
38 valley
39 mountains
40 wind

If you score …

0–24	25–31	32–40
you are unlikely to get an acceptable score under examination conditions and we recommend that you spend a lot of time improving your English before you take IELTS.	you may get an acceptable score under examination conditions but we recommend that you think about having more practice or lessons before you take IELTS.	you are likely to get an acceptable score under examination conditions but remember that different institutions will find different scores acceptable.

TEST 2

LISTENING

Section 1, Questions 1–10

1 races
2 insurance
3 Jerriz
4 25 / twenty-five
5 stadium
6 park
7 coffee
8 leader
9 route
10 lights

Section 2, Questions 11–20

11 C
12 B
13 C
14 B
15 B
16 A
17&18 *IN EITHER ORDER*
C
E
19&20 *IN EITHER ORDER*
B
D

Section 3, Questions 21–30

21 B
22 A
23 C
24 C
25 A
26 A
27 C
28 D
29 G
30 B

Section 4, Questions 31–40

31 location
32 world
33 personal
34 attention
35 name
36 network
37 frequency
38 colour / color
39 brain
40 self

If you score …

0–17	18–26	27–40
you are unlikely to get an acceptable score under examination conditions and we recommend that you spend a lot of time improving your English before you take IELTS.	you may get an acceptable score under examination conditions but we recommend that you think about having more practice or lessons before you take IELTS.	you are likely to get an acceptable score under examination conditions but remember that different institutions will find different scores acceptable.

READING

Reading Section 1, Questions 1–14

1 FALSE
2 TRUE
3 FALSE
4 TRUE
5 TRUE
6 NOT GIVEN
7 NOT GIVEN
8 C
9 D
10 D
11 A
12 B
13 C
14 A

Reading Section 2, Questions 15–27

15 expectations
16 concerns
17 report
18 dull
19 targets
20 micromanage
21 flexibility
22 unemployment
23 direction
24 suspicion
25 experience
26 graphics
27 media

Reading Section 3, Questions 28–40

28 sheep
29 shellfish
30 beak
31 rock
32 school
33 D
34 B
35 C
36 A
37 D
38 D
39 D
40 C

If you score …

0–24	25–31	32–40
you are unlikely to get an acceptable score under examination conditions and we recommend that you spend a lot of time improving your English before you take IELTS.	you may get an acceptable score under examination conditions but we recommend that you think about having more practice or lessons before you take IELTS.	you are likely to get an acceptable score under examination conditions but remember that different institutions will find different scores acceptable.

TEST 3

LISTENING

Section 1, Questions 1–10

1 850
2 bike / bicycle
3 parking
4 30 / thirty
5 weekend(s)
6 cinema
7 hospital
8 dentist
9 Thursday
10 café

Section 2, Questions 11–20

11 F
12 D
13 A
14 B
15 C
16 G
17&18 ***IN EITHER ORDER***
B
C
19&20 ***IN EITHER ORDER***
B
D

Section 3, Questions 21–30

21 C
22 A
23 A
24 B
25 C
26 F
27 H
28 D
29 A
30 E

Section 4, Questions 31–40

31 tongue(s)
32 plants
33 snakes
34 sky
35 partner(s)
36 contact
37 protection
38 tail(s)
39 steps
40 injury / injuries

If you score …

0–17	18–26	27–40
you are unlikely to get an acceptable score under examination conditions and we recommend that you spend a lot of time improving your English before you take IELTS.	you may get an acceptable score under examination conditions but we recommend that you think about having more practice or lessons before you take IELTS.	you are likely to get an acceptable score under examination conditions but remember that different institutions will find different scores acceptable.

READING

Reading Section 1, Questions 1–14

1 TRUE
2 TRUE
3 TRUE
4 NOT GIVEN
5 FALSE
6 FALSE
7 NOT GIVEN
8 E
9 F
10 D
11 C
12 D
13 A
14 G

Reading Section 2, Questions 15–27

15 law
16 equipment
17 concerns
18 breaks
19 risk
20 training
21 injuries
22 medication
23 F
24 E
25 G
26 D
27 A

Reading Section 3, Questions 28–40

28 C
29 D
30 B
31 A
32 B
33 A
34 C
35 brown
36 sunlight
37 transpiration
38 weight
39 fingers
40 moisture

If you score …

0–26	27–32	33–40
you are unlikely to get an acceptable score under examination conditions and we recommend that you spend a lot of time improving your English before you take IELTS.	you may get an acceptable score under examination conditions but we recommend that you think about having more practice or lessons before you take IELTS.	you are likely to get an acceptable score under examination conditions but remember that different institutions will find different scores acceptable.

TEST 4

LISTENING

Section 1, Questions 1–10

1 Finance
2 Maths / Math / Mathematics
3 business
4 17 / seventeen
5 holiday(s) / vacation(s)
6 college
7 location
8 jeans
9 late
10 smile

Section 2, Questions 11–20

11 A
12 B
13 A
14 C
15 A
16 B
17 B
18 D
19 A
20 E

Section 3, Questions 21–30

21 A
22 A
23 C
24 C
25 B
26 A
27&28 *IN EITHER ORDER*
B
C
29&30 *IN EITHER ORDER*
D
E

Section 4, Questions 31–40

31 destruction
32 universities / university
33 political
34 port(s)
35 slaves / slavery
36 taxation
37 sugar
38 tea
39 transportation
40 night

If you score ...

0–17	18–26	27–40
you are unlikely to get an acceptable score under examination conditions and we recommend that you spend a lot of time improving your English before you take IELTS.	you may get an acceptable score under examination conditions but we recommend that you think about having more practice or lessons before you take IELTS.	you are likely to get an acceptable score under examination conditions but remember that different institutions will find different scores acceptable.

READING

Reading Section 1, Questions 1–14

1 FALSE
2 FALSE
3 NOT GIVEN
4 TRUE
5 TRUE
6 TRUE
7 FALSE
8 TRUE
9 G
10 A
11 B
12 E
13 A
14 F

Reading Section 2, Questions 15–27

15 representatives
16 housekeeping
17 fire
18 storage
19 reporting
20 website
21 cupboard
22 costs
23 screening
24 topics
25 headset
26 software
27 rehearsal

Reading Section 3, Questions 28–40

28 B
29 E
30 B
31 D
32 A
33 D
34 FALSE
35 TRUE
36 TRUE
37 C
38 A
39 C
40 B

If you score …

0–23	24–31	32–40
you are unlikely to get an acceptable score under examination conditions and we recommend that you spend a lot of time improving your English before you take IELTS.	you may get an acceptable score under examination conditions but we recommend that you think about having more practice or lessons before you take IELTS.	you are likely to get an acceptable score under examination conditions but remember that different institutions will find different scores acceptable.

Sample answers for Writing tasks

TEST 1, WRITING TASK 1

SAMPLE ANSWER

This is an answer written by a candidate who achieved a **Band 6.0** score. Here is the examiner's comment:

> The candidate has addressed all three bullet points, though there is room for extension of each one. The tone is appropriate and the purpose of the letter is clear. Information and ideas are arranged coherently and there is effective use of cohesive devices [*Firstly* | *Additionally* | *Consequently*]. The range of vocabulary is adequate for the task and although there are errors in word choice [*expose* / express | *trans Ference* / transfer] and several spelling errors [*develope* | *recquired* | *enormuusly* | *sincerelly*], the meaning is still clear. There is a mix of simple and complex sentence forms and although there are errors in both grammar and punctuation, these do not impede communication. Extension of the main ideas, a wider resource in both vocabulary and range of grammatical structures, along with fewer errors in spelling, grammar and punctuation would lift this script above Band 6.

Dear Mr Smith,

The purpose of this letter is to expose my interest of working during half year in the company's head office.

Firstly, I would like to mention that I have developed efficiently my. Additionally I have performed accurately the role that I have been doing over the last years. Consequently, I would like to learn about other areas in the company, and I would appreciate the opportunity of being involved in new challenges.

If that could be possible. I would like to train my assistant. She could develope the tasks that I have been doing as well as me. Moreover, I can confide un her. She has a wide knowledge and the capability to develope any task related to my job. Not only she could do my job but also she could have my advice at any time that it would be recquired.

I would enormuusly appreciate if you could have the possibility of arrange overseas my trans Ference to the head office in the company.

Your sincerelly

TEST 1, WRITING TASK 2

SAMPLE ANSWER

This is an answer written by a candidate who achieved a **Band 6.5** score. Here is the examiner's comment:

> The candidate addresses all parts of the task and presents a clear position throughout the response. Main ideas are presented, supported and expanded, especially in the second paragraph. Organisation is logical and there is generally clear progression throughout, but linking within and between some sentences is occasionally faulty or weak [... *in danger. Because* ... | *commit crimes. So, bad sequences* ... | *be imposed. Because it is not good* ... | *at night, however*]. The range of vocabulary is sufficient to demonstrate some less common items and some collocations [*pros and cons* | *safe areas* | *commit crimes* | *drugs* | *rapes* | *robberies* | *exempted*]. Spelling errors are rare [*high crime late*/*rate* | *cufew*] and there are only occasional examples of incorrect word choice [*from*/some *background* | *may*/need *not be imposed in safe areas* | *area which*/where]. There is a variety of complex structures, with frequent error-free sentences. Grammar and punctuation are generally well controlled.

In some regions of America, a 'curfew' seems to be imposed although it has not been imposed in Japan for many years. There should be from background to impose a curfew and this essay will discuss pros and cons about it.

First of all, curfews may not be imposed in safe areas. Safe areas mean that the crime rate is low. If teenagers go out at night in the area which there are many crimes happening, they would be involved and be in danger. Because they do not know how to protect themselves from possible dangers of crimes. Also, it is possible that teens might commit crimes due to the fact they are curious about everything and they are easily involved to their friends. In addition, high crime late sometimes means that parents' interest about education is low. Therefore children get interested in crimes, drugs, rapes, robberies instead of studying. Consequently, children will not get good jobs and will become poor, then will commit crimes. So, bad sequences will be repeated. In such situations, it may be necessary to impose a curfew.

However, there may be a opinion that a cufew should not be imposed. Because it is not good idea to restrict children's action and children's freedom should be respected instead. I agree with this idea to some extent. If a teen is less than 15 years old, they should not be outside after 9 o'clock. However, teens over 15 years old can understand what is wrong.

In conclusion, in a dangerous area teenagers might be restricted to go out at night, however ages over 15 can be exempted. What is more important thing is to educate people including parents. Otherwise, situations will not change.

TEST 2, WRITING TASK 1

SAMPLE ANSWER

This is an answer written by a candidate who achieved a **Band 7.0** score. Here is the examiner's comment:

> This letter establishes the background to the meeting, thus creating a context for what is to follow. The purpose is clear, the tone is both consistent and appropriate (formal), and each of the bullet points is highlighted and developed. Organisation is logical and there is a clear progression throughout the response. There is also an appropriate range of cohesive devices [*According to* | *However* | *Taking into consideration* | *Considering*]. There is a sufficient range of vocabulary to allow some flexibility; there is good use of less common items and evidence of collocation [*facilities* | *hotel amenities* | *dissatisfied with* | *stale* | *tough and undercooked* | *abdominal discomfort* | *favourable reports* | *negative feedback*]. There are only occasional spelling errors. The writer uses a variety of complex structures and does so accurately, showing good control over both grammar and punctuation.

Dear Sir or Madam,

I am writing in connection with a meeting which was organised in your hotel on the 1st November for the employees of the 'Avanta' company. According to the feedback given by the guests they thoughroughly enjoyed hotel facilities, particularly the outstanding design of the building and furnishing, as well as the quality of reseption and transfer provided.

However, in spite of the overall contentment with hotel amenities the participants of the meeting reported being dissatisfied with the quality of food served for lunch. All colleagues agreed on the fact that the food was stale, especially bread and some of the salads, and the meat was tough and undercooked. One of the guests complained about having abdominal discomfort after the lunch, though not leading to any serious problems.

Taking into consideration the abovesaid, we would appreciate it if you establish a better control over the kitchen and the cooking process. Considering all favourable reports that were heard about the hotel so far we are not going to leave any negative feedback officially. We hope that this was simply a misfortunate accident and the fame of your hotel will not suffer from it.

Faithfully yours,

TEST 2, WRITING TASK 2

SAMPLE ANSWER

This is an answer written by a candidate who achieved a **Band 5.5** score. Here is the examiner's comment:

> The candidate addresses both parts of the task, but does not develop them sufficiently to achieve a higher score. Some of the response (about his/her personal experience) is not relevant. Information is presented with some organisation and there is some sense of progression, but the response would achieve a higher rating if it was better organised and used paragraphs to develop the different parts of the answer. The range of vocabulary is just about adequate for the task [*problem with weight* | *fitness club* | *GYM* | *practise sports*], but there are spelling errors in even quite simple words [*than*/then | *cheep*/cheap | *laizy*/lazy | *famoust*/famous]. The range of structures is limited, with frequent use of short, simple sentences. Complex sentences are attempted, but usually contain errors [*Now we can see a lot of people who have problem with weight.* | *I try don't give up* | *I can don't go to the GYM* | *make yourself to do something*] and this sometimes causes difficulty for the reader.

I agree, that many working people not get enough exercise, and than they have health problems. Now we can see a lot of people who have problem with weight. For example in America they have a big problem with this, but another side, they have a lot of fitness club, GYM, and it is cheep to go there. But most of them laizy to do something or they have a lot of work and have no time to practise sports I can't understand it. I think it depends on lifestyle and person. Everywhere you have to work, sometimes on a two jobs, that have money for life, for your family. But you can see for example of the famous people. Everytime they they are busy, but they find a time to practise sport. Not just famoust people, I said it depends on people. I used to practise sport. It started When I was child and I try don't give up because I like it. I can don't go to the GYM, for example, one month, but after I can't sit on the one place and do nothing. I need it, I want to be tired. And now this is my lifestyle and I think, that I never give up. What can be done, that people start to do exercise? First you have to make yourself to do something. For example, do exercise in the morning, after You need to follow what you eat. Because now people like eating fast food, they have no time to cook at home, but it does not matter. And just one day stand up and go to the gym and start to practise. And everything will be okay!

TEST 3, WRITING TASK 1

SAMPLE ANSWER

This is an answer written by a candidate who achieved a **Band 5.5** score. Here is the examiner's comment:

> This script directly addresses the requirements of the task: the purpose is clear and all the bullet points are covered adequately, in spite of some irrelevant details. The opening to, and the closure of, the letter are not appropriate however, particularly as the instructions for this task say '*Begin your letter as follows: Dear Sir or Madam,*'. Information is presented in an organised way, helped by the use of paragraphs and appropriate, if basic, cohesive devices [*Today* | *Now* | *Also*]. The range of vocabulary is just sufficient for the task, but there are noticeable spelling errors [*wos firghtened* | *deseeses*] and errors in word formation [*childs*]. There is a mixture of simple and complex sentence structures. Errors occur in some time/tense relationships [*we see*/saw | *come*/came *home from school*], but other examples of similar structures are produced correctly [*We walked out the door* | *My neighbour came out and he saw*].

Dear local authorities,

I am writing because there is a problem with the rubbish collection in my local area. The rubbish has not been emptied from the bins for three weeks and there are rats and flies all over the area.

Today I was going to take my childs school. We walked out the door and arrgh we see a BIG horrid rat. My childs screamed. I wos firghtened and I screamed. My neighbour came out from his house and he saw a big rat too. Oh no this is so bad. Today my childs come home from school but did not want to. If he can stay at school he wants to stay there to not see the rats.

Now there are so many flies. When I went to the bins I saw so many flies. They are dirty with deseeses. Also My neighbour came out and he saw the flies too.

I think you need to empty the rubbish to stop the rats and flies. If not we will get deseeses and be frightened to go out from our house. Please can you come this week and put the rubbish from my bin in to your rubbish collection truck.

Sincerely

TEST 3, WRITING TASK 2

SAMPLE ANSWER

This is an answer written by a candidate who achieved a **Band 7.0** score. Here is the examiner's comment:

> The writer addresses all parts of the task and presents a clear position throughout the response. Main ideas are put forward, and are extended and supported for each part of the task. Information and ideas are presented logically and there is a clear progression throughout the script. The writer uses a range of cohesive devices [*Also* | *this* |*In addition* | *Last year* | *all* |*too* | *this film* | *In conclusion*]. Each paragraph has a clear central topic, which supports the overall sense of progression. The range of vocabulary is sufficient to allow some flexibility [*movie theatre* | *movies*], to use less common items [*gadgets* | *popcorn*] and to show awareness of collocation [*meet up* | *big screen* | *sound quality* |*at different times and with different people*]. There are only two spelling errors [*frinds* /friends | *to gether*/together]. There is a variety of complex structures and many sentences are error free. There is also good control of punctuation.

Some people think that now we can watch movies on gadgets we do not need to attend movie theatre. Some think that to be really liked movies must be seen in a movie theatre. In this essay I will discuss both these views and give my own opinion.

To see films on our tablets and phones there is no need to go to the cinema. On my tablet I see every film I want to see. Also this way is cheap. Each month I pay £9 and I watch many films in my home or on train. If something happen I can stop and do it and later I can watch my film again. I like this and then I fully enjoy it as my stress is not there.

In addition, I like to go the cinema. I like my frinds and me to meet up and go to cinema and if I see my boyfriend I like to go to cinema to see a film to gether. Last year on my birthday many friends and me all went to cinema to gether and we watched Deep Water Horizon. I enjoyed this and my friends too, because the big screen showed more information and because the sound quality was better than at home. May be in my house we will not be so happy to watch this film and see the famous actor. Also, we enjoyed the popcorn and coke we could buy.

In conclusion in my house I like to watch films on my tablet. It is cheap and easy for me, but I also like to go to cinema to see films, especially with friends. Maybe both are good to fully enjoy films at different times and with different people.

TEST 4, WRITING TASK 1

SAMPLE ANSWER

This is an answer written by a candidate who achieved a **Band 5.0** score. Here is the examiner's comment:

> The letter does address the task, but the opening is not entirely appropriate e.g. [*Dear friend*] and nor is his introduction of himself to his friend [*Hello, my name is Vernon*]. The use of [*my friend*] as a form of address throughout the answer is also inappropriate. The bullet points are covered, but there is not much information on the last one as the writer only says [*you write him*], rather than explaining how to apply for the job. There is some organisation in the letter as each bullet point is covered in a separate paragraph, but there is little use of cohesive devices and the response is a little repetitive because of a lack of reference or substitution e.g. [*this job* | *fix computer*]. Vocabulary is fairly basic and spelling errors are noticeable [*Enginer* | *employes*]. The range of grammatical structures is limited, with frequent errors and although some complex forms are attempted, they too contain errors. Non-sentences also appear i.e. there is no verb [*Computer.* | *To fix computer.* | *9 to 5clock.*].

Dear friend

Hello my name is Vernon. How about this job for you my friend. This job in my local company that might be suitable for you. Computer Enginer. To fix computer. My friend fix computer in my local company. Daytime go to work fix computer not working which is broken. You like computer and at work fix broken computer and all employes learn fix broken computer If computer broken you fix and help employes learn fix broken computer. How about it.

I know my friend you Study computer and gradate computer May 2013. I know my friend you love computer. The work hours is so good for you my friend. 9 to 5clock. When I hear about this job, it so suitable for you. You is Computer Enginer.

My friend I suggest you to apply for the job. My boss he is kind man. Tomorrow you write him and I tell my boss you is a good man. I tell him you is Computer Enginer.

Regards

Vernon

TEST 4, WRITING TASK 2

SAMPLE ANSWER

This is an answer written by a candidate who achieved a **Band 6.5** score. Here is the examiner's comment:

> The candidate gives an extended response to the task, explaining why s/he agrees with the ideas and supporting his/her view with examples. His/her position is clear throughout and summarised briefly at the end. Information is organised logically and there is a clear progression throughout. There is some use of cohesive devices [*Furthermore* | *then* | *Sometimes* | *Also* | *To conclude*] and of reference [*this work* | *what I want* | *what I need* | *This is so terrible*], but the range is not wide. Vocabulary is generally adequate [*tidy and clean* | *in the correct situation*] and even where the word form or choice is incorrect, or spelling is faulty, the meaning is still clear e.g. [*there*/their *body* | *have his head sewen*/have stiches in this head | *non-tidy*/untidy | *I can suffer embarrassed*/embarrassment]. There is a variety of complex structures with frequent error-free sentences, though also occasional errors in the use of tenses [*a person that come*/came | *he fall*/fell *over*].

I think it is important to keep my house and my workplace tidy and clean with all things managed and in the correct situation.

Why is this? My home must be tidy to keep my families safe. If my home is tidy and electricity lines and toys and shoes and books are organised and in the correct place no one is going to fall over and do damage to there body. One day my friend Mohsin walked in his home to answer a person that come to his house door. He looked at the door. He didn't look at the floor and he fall over one shoe and then he went to hospital to have his head sewen. Furthermore, if people arrive and my house is non-tidy, then I can suffer embarrassed. My family and my friends like to see my house tidy and clean. I like to see my house clean.

My workplace must be tidy so everything is organised. If my workplace is organised I think I can do more work. I can do this work because all my time is for my work. Sometimes I go to work and all my time I have to spend looking for my work. My desk is dirty and paper is all over the top and my time is taken by looking for what I want to do and what I need to do. This is so terrible and now I think it is important to keep my workplace managed and all things in the correct situation. Also, if I need to find pens or pencils it is easy when organised.

To conclude in a nutshell keep house and workplace tidy is a good thing because I can find my things, my family like it, it is safe.

Sample answer sheets

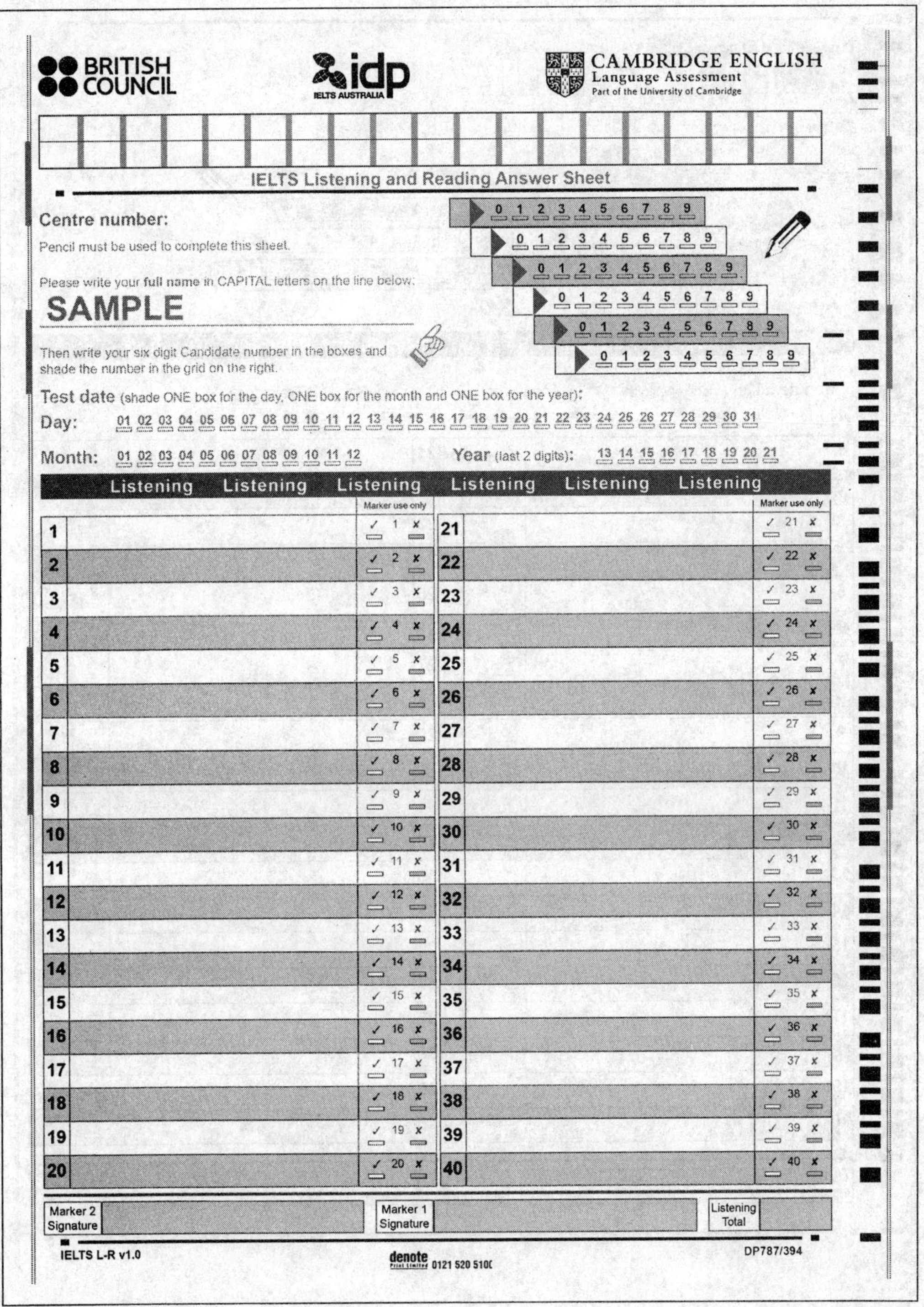

BRITISH COUNCIL

idp IELTS AUSTRALIA

CAMBRIDGE ENGLISH Language Assessment
Part of the University of Cambridge

IELTS Listening and Reading Answer Sheet

Centre number:

Pencil must be used to complete this sheet.

Please write your **full name** in CAPITAL letters on the line below:

SAMPLE

Then write your six digit Candidate number in the boxes and shade the number in the grid on the right.

0 1 2 3 4 5 6 7 8 9

0 1 2 3 4 5 6 7 8 9

0 1 2 3 4 5 6 7 8 9

0 1 2 3 4 5 6 7 8 9

0 1 2 3 4 5 6 7 8 9

0 1 2 3 4 5 6 7 8 9

Test date (shade ONE box for the day, ONE box for the month and ONE box for the year):

Day: 01 02 03 04 05 06 07 08 09 10 11 12 13 14 15 16 17 18 19 20 21 22 23 24 25 26 27 28 29 30 31

Month: 01 02 03 04 05 06 07 08 09 10 11 12 **Year** (last 2 digits): 13 14 15 16 17 18 19 20 21

Listening Listening Listening Listening Listening Listening

		Marker use only			Marker use only
1		✓ 1 ✗	21		✓ 21 ✗
2		✓ 2 ✗	22		✓ 22 ✗
3		✓ 3 ✗	23		✓ 23 ✗
4		✓ 4 ✗	24		✓ 24 ✗
5		✓ 5 ✗	25		✓ 25 ✗
6		✓ 6 ✗	26		✓ 26 ✗
7		✓ 7 ✗	27		✓ 27 ✗
8		✓ 8 ✗	28		✓ 28 ✗
9		✓ 9 ✗	29		✓ 29 ✗
10		✓ 10 ✗	30		✓ 30 ✗
11		✓ 11 ✗	31		✓ 31 ✗
12		✓ 12 ✗	32		✓ 32 ✗
13		✓ 13 ✗	33		✓ 33 ✗
14		✓ 14 ✗	34		✓ 34 ✗
15		✓ 15 ✗	35		✓ 35 ✗
16		✓ 16 ✗	36		✓ 36 ✗
17		✓ 17 ✗	37		✓ 37 ✗
18		✓ 18 ✗	38		✓ 38 ✗
19		✓ 19 ✗	39		✓ 39 ✗
20		✓ 20 ✗	40		✓ 40 ✗

Marker 2 Signature		Marker 1 Signature		Listening Total	

IELTS L-R v1.0   denote Print Limited 0121 520 510(DP787/394

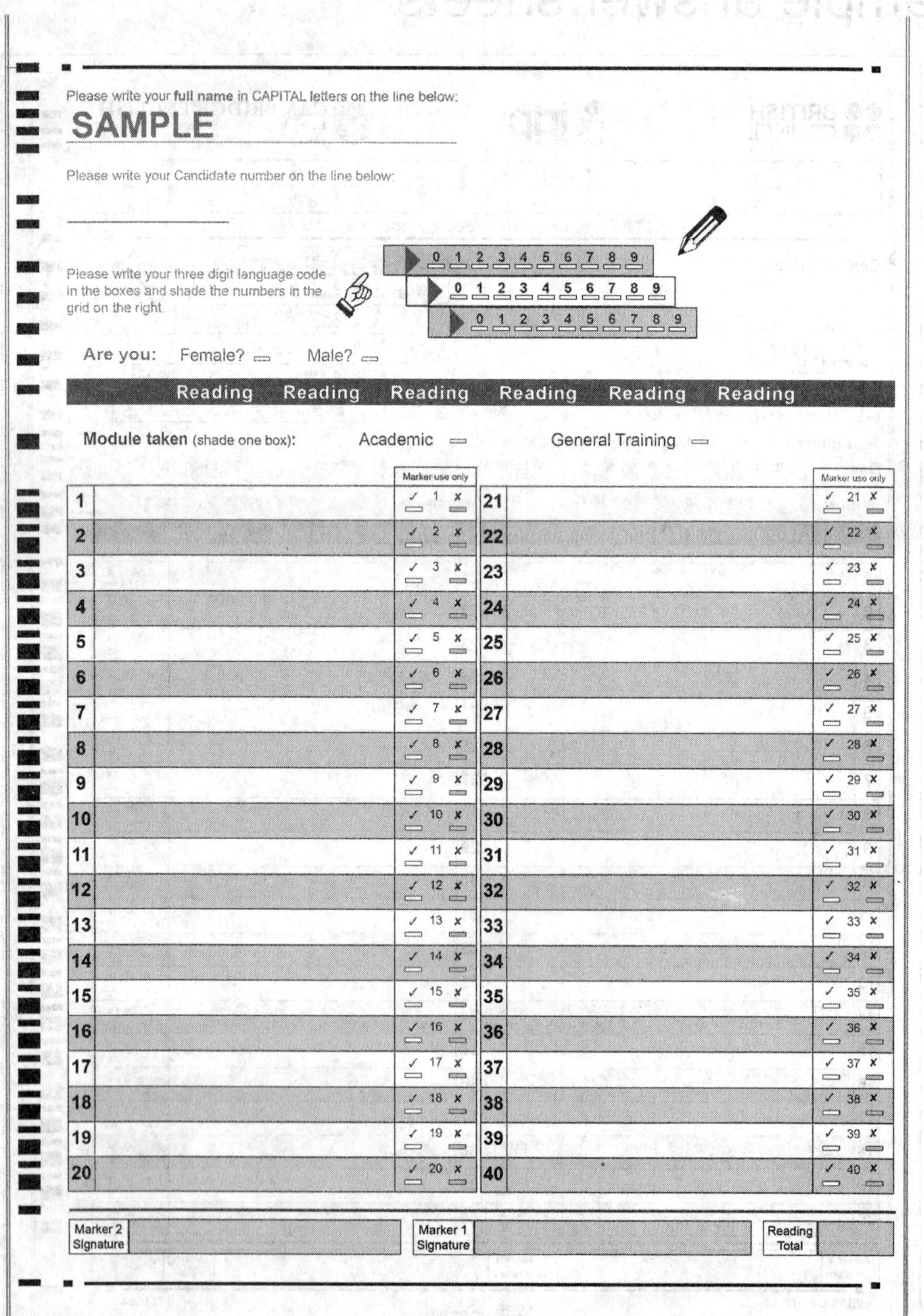

Please write your **full name** in CAPITAL letters on the line below:

SAMPLE

Please write your Candidate number on the line below:

Please write your three digit language code in the boxes and shade the numbers in the grid on the right

0 1 2 3 4 5 6 7 8 9

0 1 2 3 4 5 6 7 8 9

0 1 2 3 4 5 6 7 8 9

Are you: Female? Male?

Reading Reading Reading Reading Reading Reading

Module taken (shade one box): Academic General Training

		Marker use only			Marker use only
1		✓ 1 ✗	21		✓ 21 ✗
2		✓ 2 ✗	22		✓ 22 ✗
3		✓ 3 ✗	23		✓ 23 ✗
4		✓ 4 ✗	24		✓ 24 ✗
5		✓ 5 ✗	25		✓ 25 ✗
6		✓ 6 ✗	26		✓ 26 ✗
7		✓ 7 ✗	27		✓ 27 ✗
8		✓ 8 ✗	28		✓ 28 ✗
9		✓ 9 ✗	29		✓ 29 ✗
10		✓ 10 ✗	30		✓ 30 ✗
11		✓ 11 ✗	31		✓ 31 ✗
12		✓ 12 ✗	32		✓ 32 ✗
13		✓ 13 ✗	33		✓ 33 ✗
14		✓ 14 ✗	34		✓ 34 ✗
15		✓ 15 ✗	35		✓ 35 ✗
16		✓ 16 ✗	36		✓ 36 ✗
17		✓ 17 ✗	37		✓ 37 ✗
18		✓ 18 ✗	38		✓ 38 ✗
19		✓ 19 ✗	39		✓ 39 ✗
20		✓ 20 ✗	40		✓ 40 ✗

Marker 2 Signature		Marker 1 Signature		Reading Total	

BRITISH COUNCIL

idp IELTS AUSTRALIA

CAMBRIDGE ENGLISH Language Assessment Part of the University of Cambridge

IELTS Writing Answer Sheet – TASK 1

615290943

Candidate Name

Centre Number

Candidate Number

Module (shade one box): Academic General Training

Test date

D D M M Y Y Y Y

TASK 1

Do not write below this line

100913/2

BRITISH COUNCIL | idp IELTS AUSTRALIA | CAMBRIDGE ENGLISH Language Assessment Part of the University of Cambridge

IELTS Writing Answer Sheet – TASK 2

0181938742

Candidate Name

Centre Number | Candidate Number

Module (shade one box): Academic ▭ General Training ▭

Test date D D M M Y Y Y Y

TASK 2

Do not write below this line

100895/2

Acknowledgements

The publishers acknowledge the following sources of copyright material and are grateful for the permissions granted. While every effort has been made, it has not always been possible to identify the sources of all the material used, or to trace all copyright holders. If any omissions are brought to our notice, we will be happy to include the appropriate acknowledgements on reprinting and in the next update to the digital edition, as applicable.

Conde Nast for the text on p. 15 adapted from 'How City Living Is Reshaping the Brains and Behaviour of Urban Animals' by Brandon Keim, *Wired Magazine* 2013. Copyright © 2013 Conde Nast. Reproduced with permission; The Independent for the text on p. 16 adapted from '10 best suitcases', *The Independent*, 09.07.2013. Copyright © 2013 The Independent. Reproduced with permission; The Oxford School of Drama for the text on p. 18 adapted from 'one year acting course'. Copyright © The Oxford School of Drama. Reproduced with permission; U.S. Department of Transportation for the text on p. 20 adapted from 'Border Crossing Guide for Commercial Truck Drivers'. Reproduced under the Open Government Licence v3.0; Text on p. 22 adapted from 'Discipline and grievances at work', The Acas Guide. Copyright © Acas, Euston Tower, 286 Euston Road, London NW1 3JJ; Syon Geographical Ltd for the text on pp. 25–26 adapted from 'The world's coldest town' by Nick Middleton, *Geographical Magazine*, 01.08.2014. Copyright © 2014 Syon Geographical Ltd. Reproduced with permission; UCSF Memory and Aging Center for the text on p. 36 adapted from 'Memory', https://memory.ucsf.edu/memory. Copyright © The Regents of the University of California. Reproduced with kind permission; EasyRoommate for the text on p. 37 adapted from '1 Toronto Roommate'. Copyright © EasyRoommate. Content Provided by EasyRoommate, the web's largest online flat sharing service; TechRadar for the text on p. 39 adapted from 'Best free iPhone apps 2017' by Craig Grannell. Copyright © Future Publishing Limited. Reproduced with permission; Strategy Execution for the text on p. 41 adapted from 'How To Delegate Project Tasks' by Elizabeth Harrin. Copyright © 2014 Strategy Execution. Reproduced with kind permission; Guardian News and Media Limited for the text on p. 43 adapted from 'Functional, chronological or creative? How to choose the right CV format' by Bryn Davies, *The Guardian*, 17.08.2015. Copyright © 2015 Guardian News and Media Limited 2015. Reproduced with permission; BBC Focus for the text on pp. 45–46 adapted from 'Unsolved mysteries of the dinosaurs' by Steve Brusatte, *BBC Focus*, issue 303 – 2017. Copyright © 2017 Immediate Media Company London Ltd. Reproduced with permission; NYLSO for the text on p. 59 adapted from 'New York Late-starters String Orchestra'. Copyright © New York Late-Starters String Orchestra. Reproduced with kind permission; The Independent for the text on p. 61 adapted from 'The 10 best running watches' by Kate Hilpern, *The Independent*, 06.12.2013. Copyright © 2013 The Independent. Reproduced with permission; Nidirect government services for the text on p. 63 adapted from 'Employees' health and safety responsibilities'. Reproduced under the Open Government Licence v3.0; Nielsen-Massey Vanillas, Inc. for the text on pp. 67–68 adapted from 'The Origins of Vanilla'. Copyright © Nielsen-Massey Vanillas, Inc. Reproduced with kind permission; Guardian News and Media Limited for the text on p. 81 adapted from 'Readers' travel photography competition 2015', *The Guardian*, 19.01.2015. Copyright © 2015 Guardian News and Media Limited. Reproduced with permission; The Independent for the text on p. 83 adapted from 'The 10 Best Running headphones' by Max Benwell, *The Independent*, 30.09.2014. Copyright © 2014 The Independent. Reproduced with permission; Health and Safety Executive for the text on p. 85 adapted from 'Risk assessment for general office cleaning'. Reproduced under the Open Government Licence v3.0; Interview Success Formula for the text on p. 87 adapted from

'Preparing for a Virtual Job Interview'. Copyright © Interview Success Inc. Reproduced with permission; Warwick Business School for the text on pp. 89–90 adapted from 'Tuning up your leadership skills', *Core Magazine*. Copyright © 2013 Warwick Business School. Reproduced with kind permission.

URLS

The publisher has used its best endeavours to ensure that the URLs for external websites referred to in this book are correct and active at the time of going to press. However, the publisher has no responsibility for the websites and can make no guarantee that a site will remain live or that the content is or will remain appropriate.